YASIR ARAFAT

MENACHEM BEGIN

TONY BLAIR

GEORGE W. BUSH

JIMMY CARTER

VICENTE FOX

SADDAM HUSSEIN

HOSNI MUBARAK

VLADIMIR PUTIN

MOHAMMED REZA PAHLAVI

ANWAR SADAT

THE SAUDI ROYAL FAMILY

# Jimmy Carter

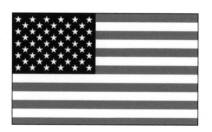

**Kerry Acker**

CHELSEA HOUSE
PUBLISHERS

A Haights Cross Communications Company

Philadelphia

**CHELSEA HOUSE PUBLISHERS**

EDITOR IN CHIEF  Sally Cheney
DIRECTOR OF PRODUCTION  Kim Shinners
CREATIVE MANAGER  Takeshi Takahashi
MANUFACTURING MANAGER  Diann Grasse

**Staff for JIMMY CARTER**

EDITOR Lee Marcott
ASSOCIATE EDITOR Patrick Stone
PRODUCTION ASSISTANT Jaimie Winkler
PICTURE RESEARCH  21st Century Publishing and Communications, Inc.
SERIES AND COVER DESIGNER  Takeshi Takahashi
LAYOUT  21st Century Publishing and Communications, Inc.

A Haights Cross Communications ✦ Company

http://www.chelseahouse.com

First Printing

1  3  5  7  9  8  6  4  2

Library of Congress Cataloging-in-Publication Data

Acker, Kerry.
  Jimmy Carter / Kerry Acker.
      p. cm.—(Major world leaders)
Summary: Profiles former peanut farmer, Georgia Governor, and United States president
Jimmy Carter, including his ongoing promotion of social justice and human rights around
the world.
Includes bibliographical references and index.
   ISBN 0-7910-6947-8
  1. Carter, Jimmy, 1924–  —Juvenile literature. 2. Presidents—United States—Biography—
Juvenile literature. [1. Carter, Jimmy, 1924–  2. Presidents.] I. Title. II. Series.
E873 .A65 2002
973.926'092—dc21
                                                                    2002008446

# TABLE OF CONTENTS

# On Leadership

## Arthur M. Schlesinger, jr.

eadership, it may be said, is really what makes the world go round. Love no doubt smoothes the passage; but love is a private transaction between consenting adults. Leadership is a public transaction with history. The idea of leadership affirms the capacity of individuals to move, inspire, and mobilize masses of people so that they act together in pursuit of an end. Sometimes leadership serves good purposes, sometimes bad; but whether the end is benign or evil, great leaders are those men and women who leave their personal stamp on history.

Now, the very concept of leadership implies the proposition that individuals can make a difference. This proposition has never been universally accepted. From classical times to the present day, eminent thinkers have regarded individuals as no more than the agents and pawns of larger forces, whether the gods and goddesses of the ancient world or, in the modern era, race, class, nation, the dialectic, the will of the people, the spirit of the times, history itself. Against such forces, the individual dwindles into insignificance.

So contends the thesis of historical determinism. Tolstoy's great novel *War and Peace* offers a famous statement of the case. Why, Tolstoy asked, did millions of men in the Napoleonic Wars, denying their human feelings and their common sense, move back and forth across Europe slaughtering their fellows? "The war," Tolstoy answered, "was bound to happen simply because it was bound to happen." All prior history determined it. As for leaders, they, Tolstoy said, "are but the labels that serve to give a name to an end and, like labels, they have the least possible connection with the event." The greater the leader, "the more conspicuous the inevitability and the predestination of every act he commits." The leader, said Tolstoy, is "the slave of history."

Determinism takes many forms. Marxism is the determinism of class. Nazism the determinism of race. But the idea of men and women as the slaves of history runs athwart the deepest human instincts. Rigid determinism abolishes the idea of human freedom—the assumption of free choice that underlies every move we make, every word we speak, every thought we think. It abolishes the idea of human responsibility, since it is manifestly unfair to reward or punish people for actions that are by definition beyond their control. No one can live consistently by any deterministic creed. The Marxist states prove this themselves by their extreme susceptibility to the cult of leadership.

More than that, history refutes the idea that individuals make no difference. In December 1931 a British politician crossing Fifth Avenue in New York City between 76th and 77th Streets around 10:30 P.M. looked in the wrong direction and was knocked down by an automobile— a moment, he later recalled, of a man aghast, a world aglare: "I do not understand why I was not broken like an eggshell or squashed like a gooseberry." Fourteen months later an American politician, sitting in an open car in Miami, Florida, was fired on by an assassin; the man beside him was hit. Those who believe that individuals make no difference to history might well ponder whether the next two decades would have been the same had Mario Constasino's car killed Winston Churchill in 1931 and Giuseppe Zangara's bullet killed Franklin Roosevelt in 1933. Suppose, in addition, that Lenin had died of typhus in Siberia in 1895 and that Hitler had been killed on the western front in 1916. What would the 20th century have looked like now?

For better or for worse, individuals do make a difference. "The notion that a people can run itself and its affairs anonymously," wrote the philosopher William James, "is now well known to be the silliest of absurdities. Mankind does nothing save through initiatives on the part of inventors, great or small, and imitation by the rest of us—these are the sole factors in human progress. Individuals of genius show the way, and set the patterns, which common people then adopt and follow."

Leadership, James suggests, means leadership in thought as well as in action. In the long run, leaders in thought may well make the greater difference to the world. "The ideas of economists and political philosophers, both when they are right and when they are wrong," wrote John Maynard Keynes, "are more powerful than is commonly understood. Indeed the world is ruled by little else. Practical men, who believe themselves to be quite exempt from any intellectual influences, are usually the slaves of some defunct economist. . . . The power of vested interests is vastly exaggerated compared with the gradual encroachment of ideas."

But, as Woodrow Wilson once said, "Those only are leaders of men, in the general eye, who lead in action. . . . It is at their hands that new thought gets its translation into the crude language of deeds." Leaders in thought often invent in solitude and obscurity, leaving to later generations the tasks of imitation. Leaders in action—the leaders portrayed in this series—have to be effective in their own time.

And they cannot be effective by themselves. They must act in response to the rhythms of their age. Their genius must be adapted, in a phrase from William James, "to the receptivities of the moment." Leaders are useless without followers. "There goes the mob," said the French politician, hearing a clamor in the streets. "I am their leader. I must follow them." Great leaders turn the inchoate emotions of the mob to purposes of their own. They seize on the opportunities of their time, the hopes, fears, frustrations, crises, potentialities. They succeed when events have prepared the way for them, when the community is awaiting to be aroused, when they can provide the clarifying and organizing ideas. Leadership completes the circuit between the individual and the mass and thereby alters history.

It may alter history for better or for worse. Leaders have been responsible for the most extravagant follies and most monstrous crimes that have beset suffering humanity. They have also been vital in such gains as humanity has made in individual freedom, religious and racial tolerance, social justice, and respect for human rights.

There is no sure way to tell in advance who is going to lead for good and who for evil. But a glance at the gallery of men and women in MAJOR WORLD LEADERS suggests some useful tests.

One test is this: Do leaders lead by force or by persuasion? By command or by consent? Through most of history leadership was exercised by the divine right of authority. The duty of followers was to defer and to obey. "Theirs not to reason why/Theirs but to do and die." On occasion, as with the so-called enlightened despots of the 18th century in Europe, absolutist leadership was animated by humane purposes. More often, absolutism nourished the passion for domination, land, gold, and conquest and resulted in tyranny.

The great revolution of modern times has been the revolution of equality. "Perhaps no form of government," wrote the British historian James Bryce in his study of the United States, *The American Commonwealth*, "needs great leaders so much as democracy." The idea that all people should be equal in their legal condition has undermined the old structure of authority, hierarchy, and deference. The revolution of equality has had two contrary effects on the nature of leadership. For equality, as Alexis de Tocqueville pointed out in his great study *Democracy in America*, might mean equality in servitude as well as equality in freedom.

"I know of only two methods of establishing equality in the political world," Tocqueville wrote. "Rights must be given to every citizen, or none at all to anyone . . . save one, who is the master of all." There was no middle ground "between the sovereignty of all and the absolute power of one man." In his astonishing prediction of 20th-century totalitarian dictatorship, Tocqueville explained how the revolution of equality could lead to the *Führerprinzip* and more terrible absolutism than the world had ever known.

But when rights are given to every citizen and the sovereignty of all is established, the problem of leadership takes a new form, becomes more exacting than ever before. It is easy to issue commands and enforce them by the rope and the stake, the concentration camp and the *gulag*. It is much harder to use argument and achievement to overcome opposition and win consent. The Founding Fathers of the United States understood the difficulty. They believed that history had given them the opportunity to decide, as Alexander Hamilton wrote in the first Federalist Paper, whether men are indeed capable of basing government on "reflection and choice, or whether they are forever destined to depend . . . on accident and force."

Government by reflection and choice called for a new style of leadership and a new quality of followership. It required leaders to be responsive to popular concerns, and it required followers to be active and informed participants in the process. Democracy does not eliminate emotion from politics; sometimes it fosters demagoguery; but it is confident that, as the greatest of democratic leaders put it, you cannot fool all of the people all of the time. It measures leadership by results and retires those who overreach or falter or fail.

It is true that in the long run despots are measured by results too. But they can postpone the day of judgment, sometimes indefinitely, and in the meantime they can do infinite harm. It is also true that democracy is no guarantee of virtue and intelligence in government, for the voice of the people is not necessarily the voice of God. But democracy, by assuring the right of opposition, offers built-in resistance to the evils inherent in absolutism. As the theologian Reinhold Niebuhr summed it up, "Man's capacity for justice makes democracy possible, but man's inclination to justice makes democracy necessary."

A second test for leadership is the end for which power is sought. When leaders have as their goal the supremacy of a master race or the promotion of totalitarian revolution or the acquisition and exploitation of colonies or the protection of greed and privilege or the preservation of personal power, it is likely that their leadership will do little to advance the cause of humanity. When their goal is the abolition of slavery, the liberation of women, the enlargement of opportunity for the poor and powerless, the extension of equal rights to racial minorities, the defense of the freedoms of expression and opposition, it is likely that their leadership will increase the sum of human liberty and welfare.

Leaders have done great harm to the world. They have also conferred great benefits. You will find both sorts in this series. Even "good" leaders must be regarded with a certain wariness. Leaders are not demigods; they put on their trousers one leg after another just like ordinary mortals. No leader is infallible, and every leader needs to be reminded of this at regular intervals. Irreverence irritates leaders but is their salvation. Unquestioning submission corrupts leaders and demeans followers. Making a cult of a leader is always a mistake. Fortunately hero worship generates its own antidote. "Every hero," said Emerson, "becomes a bore at last."

The signal benefit the great leaders confer is to embolden the rest of us to live according to our own best selves, to be active, insistent, and resolute in affirming our own sense of things. For great leaders attest to the reality of human freedom against the supposed inevitabilities of history. And they attest to the wisdom and power that may lie within the most unlikely of us, which is why Abraham Lincoln remains the supreme example of great leadership. A great leader, said Emerson, exhibits new possibilities to all humanity. "We feed on genius . . . . Great men exist that there may be greater men."

Great leaders, in short, justify themselves by emancipating and empowering their followers. So humanity struggles to master its destiny, remembering with Alexis de Tocqueville: "It is true that around every man a fatal circle is traced beyond which he cannot pass; but within the wide verge of that circle he is powerful and free; as it is with man, so with communities." ∎

Jimmy Carter may have had a difficult four-year term in the White House, but his integrity and humanitarian achievements have never been questioned. In this 1996 photograph, Carter holds his Lions Humanitarian Award, which he received at the 79th Lions International Convention in Montreal, Canada, for his creation of the Carter Center.

# 1

# Jimmy Carter's Legacy

"All I want is the same thing you want: to have a nation with a government that is as good, and honest, and decent, and competent, and compassionate, and as filled with love as are the American people."
—CARTER TO VOTERS IN SACRAMENTO, MAY 20, 1976

W hen Jimmy Carter first announced his candidacy for the presidency in 1975, Americans knew almost nothing about the earnest peanut farmer and one-term governor of Georgia. Few people really took the man with the kind smile and Southern drawl very seriously at the beginning of the Democratic race. But after organizing an extraordinary grass-roots campaign, winning 18 primary elections, and becoming the Democratic nominee, Carter went on to defeat incumbent President Gerald R. Ford in the 1976 election. Remarkably, Jimmy Carter had risen from

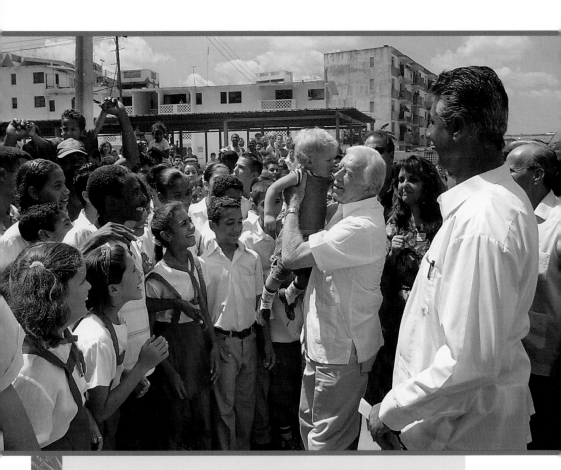

Carter's historic journey to Cuba in May of 2002, at the invitation of Cuba's President Fidel Castro, continued his work to restore relations between that country and the U.S. The trip required special permission from Washington and made Carter the highest-ranked U.S. official to visit Cuba since its 1959 revolution.

near-obscurity to hold the highest office in the United States.

During his years at the White House, Carter sought to be a "president for the people." He tried to eliminate much of the pageantry and bureaucratic excess of the office. He also signed the Panama Canal treaties and normalized diplomatic relations with the People's Republic of China. Carter passed some important legislation on wilderness preservation and energy conservation.

His most significant success was indisputably his brokering of the Camp David Accord, the historic peace treaty between longtime enemies Israel and Egypt.

But Carter's administration was severely hampered by communication difficulties with Congress, a faltering economy, and an energy crisis. Also, relations between the United States and the Soviet Union were strained, particularly after the Soviets invaded Afghanistan. Carter's presidency was further damaged when 50 Americans were held hostage by revolutionaries in Iran. After months of fruitless negotiations, President Carter approved a rescue mission that ended in a humiliating failure, ultimately costing him the 1980 election.

Yet Jimmy Carter has proven himself to be an astonishingly effective former president. The traits that have always inspired respect—compassion, honesty, and integrity—now shine brighter than ever. His tireless peacekeeping efforts, relief missions, work on behalf of Habitat for Humanity, and promotion of social justice and human rights all over the world have set a new standard for ex-presidential conduct. It is in this role—as a leader in retirement—that he may leave his most enduring legacy.

Carter's mother, Lillian, holds the future president in her lap in March of 1925. Lillian Carter's sense of social justice had a profound impact on her son, who later carried her ideals into the Georgia governor's mansion and the White House.

2

# A Plains Childhood

The tiny town of Plains, in Sumter County, Georgia, located 190 miles west of Savannah and 119 miles south of Atlanta, sits on land that is extremely flat and fertile. The immediate surrounding area is mostly red-clay farmland rich in nutrients, where crops such as corn, peanuts, and cotton are cultivated. When James Earl Carter Jr. was born in 1924, there were fewer than 700 people living in Plains. It was a peaceful, hardworking community, where daily life revolved around farming, family, church, and school. This rural, humble upbringing was to have a tremendous effect on the development of Jimmy Carter's character and political philosophy. And like many of his forebears, Jimmy maintained a strong connection to the land that played such a profound role in shaping him.

The Carters' Georgian roots run deep. The family has been

in the United States since the 1640s, and state historical records indicate that some Carter family members acquired land in Georgia in the early 1800s. Wiley Carter, Jimmy's great-great-grandfather, owned land just a few miles north of Plains, then known as "the Plains of Dura"; Littleberry Walker Carter, Jimmy's great-grandfather, volunteered for the Sumter Flying Artillery during the Civil War. After the South surrendered, Littleberry returned home to work on his farm, situated just east of Americus, a town not far from Plains.

Jimmy's grandfather, William Archibald ("Billy") Carter, was born in 1858. Like his son, Earl, and future-president grandson Jimmy, Billy was highly ambitious and not afraid to earn a living through the sweat of his brow; he eventually became a successful businessman. He owned a store, three sawmills, a cotton gin, and 400 acres of land in Georgia. He also built a schoolhouse and ran a vineyard, selling thousands of gallons of wine each year.

Billy's son Earl Carter (1894–1953), the father of the future president, met Bessie Lillian Gordy (1898–1983) while she was training to be a nurse at Wise Hospital in Plains. After dating for a year, Earl and Lillian were married in 1923. About a year later, on October 1, 1924, Lillian gave birth to James Earl Carter Jr., whom they called Jimmy. He was the oldest of four children. Jimmy had two sisters, Gloria (1926–1990) and Ruth (1929–1983), and a brother, William (1937–1988), or Billy, who was named after his grandfather.

## LIFE ON THE FARM

When Jimmy was four years old, the family moved from Plains to the smaller town of Archery, only a few miles away. This was the site of the Carter family's farm, where Earl, known around the community as "Mr. Earl," also ran a farm products store. Although Earl specialized in peanut farming,

Growing up on a farm in rural Georgia taught Jimmy Carter the value of hard work. The Depression years were tough on the family, and Carter, seen here riding his pony, Lady, on his Plains farm, became quite an entrepreneur. Even at the early age of nine, he invested money and operated a series of small businesses.

he grew cotton, sugar, corn, watermelon, and potatoes, too. The young family lived in a small, square, six-room wooden clapboard house with no electricity (fireplaces provided heat), and no indoor plumbing (chamber pots were in each bedroom, and a well outside supplied the Carters with water).

There was a screened porch in the back, and also a porch in the front, where the family spent most of their leisure time together when the weather was warm. Lillian cooked meals on a wood-burning stove, and the family read at the dinner table by kerosene lamp until 1938, when electricity arrived in the area. The Carters didn't have running water until 1935, when Earl erected a windmill, purchased from a mail-order catalog, to pump water from a well.

As with other farm families, the Carter children were taught to help out with the chores. Jimmy, Gloria, Ruth, and Billy learned to work hard at a very young age. The bell rang at four o'clock in the morning, summoning all the people that worked on the farm. Jimmy ate a hearty breakfast with his family, then he and his father gathered the mules and all of the equipment with some of the other workers. He harnessed the mules to the wagons and drove out with his father to the fields.

Since there was no machinery on the Carter farm, all of the labor was done manually. Jimmy learned how to plow the soil using mules and work the crops with hoes. When he was older, he sharpened tools, fertilized crops, picked cotton, milked cows, pruned watermelons plants, and performed some carpentry and blacksmithing tasks. One of his least favorite duties was "mopping" cotton. This procedure entailed mixing water, arsenic, and molasses, and, using a rag and a stick, coating buds of cotton with the messy goo to poison the boll weevils that tried to attack the cotton. Inevitably, Jimmy's trousers would end up covered in the syrupy mixture, attracting a swarm of flies.

When Jimmy was done with his work in the fields, at sundown, he would return to the house, where he'd pump water by hand and carry it from the well. Then he fed the tired mules and chopped or sawed the wood that was used to heat the house. The Carters also raised chickens, so Jimmy and his siblings fed them and collected their eggs. Jimmy was also often responsible for catching and slaughtering the chickens that would be served for dinner.

It was a life of discipline, and it was lived simply and frugally. Though the family was not wealthy by typical standards, they were very fortunate compared to many of their neighbors. Jimmy was a young boy when the Great Depression began in 1929. The American economy collapsed, resulting in the failure of many businesses and banks. Hungry people waited in long lines to get food. Although the Depression hit farmers particularly hard, Earl managed to keep his farm going.

## "HOT SHOT" JIMMY

Earl Carter's work ethic and emphasis on responsibility and self-reliance deeply influenced Jimmy.

Mr. Earl was an exceptionally industrious man. In addition to running the farm and the store, he produced and sold his own milk, ketchup, honey, and syrup. He also was a church deacon, and a school board and hospital board member. Earl taught Jimmy to be a smart businessman, and his example encouraged his young son. At six years old, the sandy-haired boy, nicknamed "Hot" (for "hot shot") by his father, was already an entrepreneur. On the days when he wasn't working in the fields, he was selling boiled peanuts to the people of Plains. Jimmy would pull up the peanuts, shake them out, and wash them. After he and his mother boiled them and placed them in paper bags, Jimmy loaded them into his wagon, pulled it into town, and sold the treats. This venture earned him about $1 on every weekday and $5 on Saturdays.

Another example of his business acumen was demonstrated when he was nine. Jimmy purchased five bales of cotton at five cents a pound and then stored them for a few years until their value increased to eighteen cents a pound. Then he sold them. The money that he made from

Carter as a boy with his father, Earl, and sisters, Ruth and Gloria. Although Carter loved and respected his father, there was a distance between them that was not fully bridged until just before Earl Carter died of pancreatic cancer.

this transaction enabled him, eventually, to purchase five houses, which he rented out until he sold them in 1949. When Jimmy was 10 years old, he went into business with his cousin Hugh. The two sold scrap iron and old newspapers. They even sold ice cream, hot dogs, and burgers for five cents each.

Earl was a stern disciplinarian, and none of the children disobeyed the decisions made by their father. Young Jimmy was always trying to please him. "I do not remember . . . his ever saying a complimentary word to me . . . ," Carter later said. "We feared and respected him and strove to please him." But Earl did do some nice things for his son. For example, he took Jimmy hunting with him, and they shot quail and other game. He also fished for largemouth bass with his son and played baseball with him.

## JIMMY LEARNS TO BE OPEN-MINDED

Lillian Carter profoundly influenced her eldest son, too, though in an entirely different way. She had a reputation in the community for ignoring the racial segregation that prevailed in the South in the early 20th century. At a time when blacks were still using the back door to enter the homes of white families, Miss Lillian, as she was affectionately known, encouraged them to use the front door. On the other hand, Earl Carter treated his black farm workers kindly but never socialized with them. And when black people visited Lillian or his children, he'd leave the premises. Most Southerners of the time, even the most open-minded of them, still looked upon black people as second-class citizens, and they continued to segregate them. But Miss Lillian treated everybody the same. Her strong Christian beliefs led her to be "color-blind" as a nurse, in dealing with patients. She gave her black patients the same amount of care and compassion that she offered her white patients. Miss Lillian devoted much of her time to ministering to the many poverty-stricken families that lived nearby. "When Mama was home," Carter later said, "we never turned away anyone who came to our back door asking for food or a drink of water." Lillian's lack of prejudice and equal treatment of others, regardless of their color or economic status, had a considerable effect on her son and his social conscience. "More than anyone else, my mother made me see the inequities around us," he wrote.

Since there were only two white families in Archery when Jimmy was a child (of the 27 families that lived there, 25 were black), most of his childhood playmates were black. They were the sons of tenant families on the Carter farm. Jimmy was also close to Jack Clark, the Carters' black foreman, and his wife, Rachel, who worked on the farm. "Except in my own room in our house," Carter recalled, "[the Clark house] is where I felt most at home." His childhood was spent living in two worlds: one white, the other black. Carter has said that, as a farm boy, he "spoke two languages." With black friends, he said "rid" instead of "rode," and "holp" instead of "help," while "himself" became "hisself". An African-American boy named Alonzo Davis, or "A.D.," was Jimmy's closest friend. Jimmy swam, fished, invented games, wrestled, and rode his Shetland pony with A.D., and when they were teenagers, they went to the movies together. But A.D. sat in the "colored" section, while Jimmy sat in the "white" section. Carter wrote, "I don't remember ever questioning the mandatory racial separation, which we accepted like breathing."

Carter was raised in a very religious household and community. Baptized into the First Baptist Church of Plains when he was 11, he attended a Sunday school taught by his father, a deacon. Every day at school started with a chapel service. Even the parties that Jimmy went to as a teenager were sponsored by the church. The highlight of religious life in Plains was the yearly revival week, when guest evangelical preachers arrived to conduct meetings of intense and lively worship. Jimmy's parents were devout, and their children were raised to be good, wholesome Christians, committed to basic moral values. Jimmy's spiritual views were further molded by other role models, such as his friend A.D.'s mother, Rachel Clark. "Much more than my parents . . . ," Carter said, "[Clark] talked to me about the religious and moral values that shaped a person's life."

## SCHOOL DAYS

Beginning at the age of six, Carter was educated in the Plains public school system. The school was very small; all grades through high school were taught in the same building. Carter was a bright student, and his grades were always among the best in his class. Miss Lillian taught him how to read when he was four, so he had no difficulty with literature and writing. In fact, he read more than any of his classmates—during meals, in his tree house, in bed at night, almost always. He even read Leo Tolstoy's *War and Peace* when he was just 12, and he has read the book several times over the years since then.

The school superintendent, Julia Coleman, was Carter's favorite teacher. She encouraged him to read, taught him about art and music, and pushed him to enter spelling bees and school debates. Carter also memorized long poems and Bible passages. His favorite subjects were literature and history. He also played baseball and basketball, though he claims that he did not excel at either. But he did do well running track for the Plains High School team.

In Carter's senior year of high school, he was first in his class and was supposed to have been the valedictorian. However, a couple of days before graduation he and a few friends skipped school, believing that no one would find out. But Carter was caught, and his disobedience caused him to be banned from giving the valedictory speech. Nevertheless, Julia Coleman did allow him to deliver another special speech.

Carter later said he wasn't much of an athlete, but in school he participated in track, baseball, and basketball. Here he is with the Plains High School basketball team about the year 1940.

While Carter was finishing up high school, much more important events were happening in the larger world beyond Plains. The year was 1941. Europe was under attack by Germany's Adolf Hitler, and the United States was deliberating over whether or not the nation should go to war.

The decision of going to war was a less difficult one for the young Carter, however. Since grammar school, he had loved reading and learning about the Navy. Carter would eagerly await the arrival of letters and postcards from his uncle Tom Gordy, who had been a sailor in the U.S. Navy since he was young. Carter was enthralled by his Uncle Tom's stories of the South Pacific and all his exotic overseas adventures. He kept close track of Tom's travels and dreamed about becoming a sailor himself. It was a dream that would soon come true.

From the time he was a young boy and heard of his Uncle Tom's sailing adventures in exotic locales, Carter dreamed of joining the U.S. Navy. With good grades and his father's prodding of their local senator, Carter got an appointment to Annapolis. This accomplishment was also important because it helped pay for Carter's college education.

# 3

# The Navy Years

"**F**rom the time I was five years old," Carter wrote, "I would always say that someday I would be going to Annapolis, and would become a naval officer." It was a goal that was fully supported by his parents. No one in the Carter family had ever finished college, or even high school. Even Earl Carter had attended school only through the tenth grade. Jimmy took this goal very seriously, and his parents did, too. But he feared that his flat feet would prevent him from ever getting accepted into Annapolis and the Navy. So, when he was 13, he started standing on soda bottles and rolling back and forth to build up his arches. And if Jimmy was less than diligent with his schoolwork, his parents would remind him, "You'll never go to Annapolis this way!"

As Carter approached his high school graduation, "the Naval

Academy became almost an obsession in our family," he wrote. The Carters didn't have much money, and the U.S. Naval Academy in Annapolis, Maryland, would provide a free education. But the only way he could get into the school was to receive an appointment from a local congressman or U.S. senator. So Earl concentrated on winning over their congressman, Steven Pace. He also broadened his circle of friends, determined to do whatever he could to get his son the appointment. At least once every year while Jimmy was in high school, Earl took him over to the Pace home and boasted about Jimmy's academic record and achievements.

## THE NAVAL ACADEMY AT ANNAPOLIS

After Carter graduated from high school in 1941, he enrolled at Georgia Southwestern College in nearby Americus. Here, he took a course in chemistry that had not been offered in his little Plains high school. The class was recommended for admission to the Naval Academy. While he was at Georgia Southwestern, he studied engineering and chemistry, doing well in both subjects. In addition to his course work, Carter also played basketball. He then matriculated at the Georgia Institute of Technology, where he joined the Navy Reserve Officer Training Corp (ROTC) and adhered to a very strict schedule of physical training. Carter took classes in engineering, navigation, and other military sciences, and he was in the top 10% of his class. Finally, in 1943, when Carter was 19 years old, Congressman Pace delivered. Carter received his congressional appointment to Annapolis, and his lifelong dream became a reality.

When Carter started out at the academy, he had a reputation for being a "nice guy" who was always smiling. But, like every other freshman at Annapolis, he was hazed by upperclassmen. The freshmen, or "plebes," were subjected to torment and embarrassment, but Carter's hard work and steadfastness helped him through the rough times. He was a diligent student, excelling particularly in gunnery, naval tactics, and electronics. He also learned how to fly planes.

## CARTER MEETS ROSALYNN

The rules at Annapolis were rigid, and the schedule was very demanding, so all of the cadets anxiously looked forward to their time away from campus on leave. One leave in particular would stand out for Jimmy Carter. At the end of his junior year, in 1945, Jimmy was at home in Plains when his sister Ruth brought over her best friend, Rosalynn Smith. Although the Smith family had known the Carters for years (Rosalynn's sister was even named after Jimmy's mother), Jimmy had never really had a conversation with Rosalynn, and he never realized how pretty she was. Rosalynn was three years younger than he was, and Jimmy had never paid any attention to his little sister's playmate. But this time he noticed her. So Jimmy asked her to go on a date with him.

Rosalynn's upbringing was very similar to Jimmy's. Her mother worked in the Plains Post Office, and her father was a garage mechanic. When Rosalynn was just 13 years old, her father died, and she took a part-time job cleaning at a local beauty shop to help support her mother and three siblings. Like Jimmy, Rosalynn was raised to value family, hard work, religion, and community.

Rosalynn was a college student at Americus when she and Jimmy first went out. After going to the movies on their first date, Jimmy's mother asked him what he thought of Rosalynn. Jimmy said, "She's the one I want to marry." They started to write letters to each other and they would go out on dates when he was at home on leave. When Jimmy first proposed to her, on George Washington's birthday

Carter at the U.S. Naval Academy at Annapolis. The inscription is to Rosalynn Smith, whom Carter knew he wanted to marry from their first date. She postponed their engagement in order to complete her studies.

weekend, she refused because she wanted to finish all four years of college before she started a family. But the second time he proposed marriage, while she was visiting him at Annapolis in June of 1946, the year of Jimmy's graduation, Rosalynn accepted. A month later, on July 7, Rosalynn and Jimmy were married at Plains Baptist Church. Rosalynn was 19 years old, and Jimmy was 22. He had just graduated 59th out of a class of 820, and had been commissioned as an ensign for the U.S. Navy.

## CARTER'S NAVAL ASSIGNMENTS

Carter's career in the Navy began on battleships, and he spent many long weeks at sea away from Rosalynn. He was given duty on the USS *New York*, a ship stationed in the North Atlantic when World War II ended. After the war, Carter was sent to Norfolk, Virginia, where he was assigned to the USS *Wyoming*. The *Wyoming* was an older battleship that had been converted into a laboratory for testing new electronics and gunnery equipment. Carter served as a radar officer, and he taught others about electronics. He also developed a keen ability to identify ships and planes. His next assignment was aboard the USS *Mississippi*, another floating experimental station, where he served as a training and education officer. Towards the end of his stay on the *Mississippi*, Carter applied to a submarine training program. Submarine service was the Navy's most challenging and dangerous duty, but Carter was accepted into the program, and he began classes in June of 1948.

The program took place at the U.S. Navy Submarine School, located in New London, Connecticut. When Jimmy and Rosalynn moved there, they took along a new son, John William (nicknamed Jack), who was born on July 3, 1947. The family spent the next six months in Connecticut until Carter completed his coursework. When he graduated from the school in 1948, he was ranked third in a class of 52.

Carter was next stationed on the USS *Pomfret*, which was based in the Pacific. While the family moved back to Plains, Jimmy flew out to Pearl Harbor, Hawaii, where he was to begin his first assignment aboard a submarine. In January of 1949, the *Pomfret* departed the base for a simulated war patrol to China. The crossing to the Far East was rough, and Carter often stood watch holding a bucket in case he threw up! He also had a near-death experience on the *Pomfret*. The submarine, while above the water's surface, was recharging batteries when a violent storm hit. An enormous wave knocked Carter into the ocean, separating him from the submarine. He swam and swam, until he grabbed onto a cannon barrel and held on. Finally, help arrived, and he was lowered onto the deck.

The sub arrived back in Pearl Harbor on March 25. While aboard the *Pomfret*, Carter had served in many different roles, including stints as a communications officer, a gunnery officer, a sonar officer, and a supply officer. In June of 1949, he was promoted to lieutenant, junior grade.

## ABOARD THE *K-1* AND *SEA WOLF*

In February of 1951, Jimmy started a new assignment as senior engineering officer for the construction of the USS *K-1*, a submarine that was designed especially for anti-submarine warfare. When the *K-1* was completed and commissioned, he became executive officer, soon thereafter qualifying to assume total command of the sub. He was in charge of overseeing engineering, operations, and maintenance.

While Carter was aboard the *K-1*, an event occurred that illustrates how much his character had developed since childhood, and how Miss Lillian's example had influenced her son. When the *K-1* was docked in Jamaica, British officials invited some crewmembers to a party. But there was a catch: only the white crewmembers were invited. Carter's sensitivity to racial discrimination had grown

After his graduation from the Naval Academy, Carter served on several ships before becoming an officer on the submarine USS *K-1*. Already an experienced engineer, Carter would also later serve on the nuclear-powered submarine *Sea Wolf*, which helped to spur his interest in nuclear physics.

acutely since the days when he was a youth in Plains, and when he saw how deeply ingrained this discrimination was in the Navy, he felt compelled to do something about it. At Carter's urging, the *K-1* crew voted unanimously to refuse the invitation to the party. He was proud of his actions, and Carter would continue to fight prejudice, racial and otherwise, throughout his life.

In 1952, while Carter was still with the *K-1*, U.S. naval history was being made, and Carter was about to become a part of it. The Navy was attempting to develop the world's first nuclear-powered submarine. The entire program was spearheaded by a man named Hyman Rickover. Captain Rickover, who would soon rise to become Admiral Rickover, was known to be demanding, brilliant, and tough—traits that he shared with Earl Carter. Rickover, now considered the "father of the nuclear Navy," was another man who would influence Jimmy Carter profoundly.

Carter applied for a position with the atomic submarine division of the Bureau of Ships, headed by Rickover. During the interview with Rickover, Carter faced a barrage of difficult questions. Rickover, for example, grilled him about his performance at Annapolis, asking him, "Did you do your best?" Carter considered this question, and offered Rickover an honest answer: "No sir, I didn't always do my best." Rickover then quickly asked, "Why not?" Although Rickover accepted Carter into the elite program, the question ate away at the future president for years to come because he had no real answer. During the years Carter spent working with his new mentor, he plunged into his work and read extensively about mathematics, nuclear physics, and the latest technology. Rickover pushed and prodded him to excel and to do his very best, leading Carter to eventually say, "I think, second to my own father, Rickover had more effect on my life than any other man."

In June of 1952, Carter reported for duty at the U.S Atomic Energy Commission in Schenectady, New York. By this time a lieutenant, senior grade, he did graduate work in physics at Union College. Carter then went to Washington, where he assisted with the research and development of nuclear submarines. In 1953 he was assigned to an engineering officer position on the crew of the nuclear submarine *Sea Wolf*.

Throughout his years in the Navy Carter had been fully intent on becoming the chief of naval operations. But something happened in late 1952 that would change the course of his life forever. He found out that his father, then 58 years old, was dying of pancreatic cancer.

Carter originally planned a career in the Navy, but his life changed
when his father, Earl, died of cancer. Carter took over the family's
farm and, although the first few years were tough, eventually turned
the peanut farm into a successful business.

# 4

# Peanut Farmer and Civic Leader

W hen Carter first learned that his father was ill, he took an extended leave of absence and spent many hours at Earl's bedside. The two of them talked a lot—about farming and about events in the community, and, as Earl had just been elected to the Georgia House of Representatives, about politics. Carter also chatted with the many, many people visited the ailing man. He heard stories about his father's goodness, and he was particularly surprised at how generous Earl had been to his poor black neighbors. Earl Carter, though a strict segregationist, had bought graduation gowns for impoverished African-American students, donated money for some of them to attend college, and dismissed some payments that his black tenants owed him. Carter saw that his father was widely admired in Plains. "His accomplishments and the breadth of his interests were astonishing to me," he wrote. "In almost all facets of community life he was a respected leader, including education, health, agriculture, social affairs, and in his newly elected position as a member of the state legislature."

## TAKING OVER THE FAMILY FARM

When Earl Carter died on July 23, 1953, at age 59, his son did some serious thinking. He was beginning to see his father's life as more meaningful than the one Jimmy would have if he continued his career in the Navy. "Now I felt besieged by an unwelcome comparison of the ultimate value of my life with his," Carter wrote. He felt a responsibility to his community, and he believed that he was needed to assume the leadership role that his father had left behind. Yet Rosalynn did not want to return to Plains, and she argued with him about it. Carter has said that this was the "first really serious argument in our marriage."

The couple ultimately decided that Carter would resign from the Navy, and they packed up their belongings and returned to their hometown, where he would take control of the Carter family farm and Earl's peanut warehouse, located in the center of town. They brought along with them their son Jack and his two young brothers, James Earl III (nicknamed Chip), who was born on April 12, 1950, and Donnel Jeffrey (Jeff), who was born on August 18, 1952.

Because 11 years had passed since Carter had worked on a farm, he felt he had to become more educated about the latest agricultural techniques and equipment. So he approached the situation as he approached most other challenges—he talked to people, gathered as much information as possible, and read. He plunged into the operation, and took business and modern farming courses at the Agricultural Experiment Station in Tifton, Georgia.

Carter chose to concentrate on peanut farming, and he also expanded the warehouse. He purchased new farming machinery, including a peanut sheller. Carter Warehouses evolved into a general-purposes seed and farm supply company, and Carter started selling fertilizer as well. Lillian Carter and Jimmy's brother, Billy, helped him manage and operate the business, while Rosalynn handled the accounting. They sometimes put in 18 hours a day.

The first few years were difficult. There was a drought, and many area farmers were unable to sell crops. Some of those farmers owed the Carters money from purchases they had made before the drought, and they couldn't pay them back. Carter wrote about those tough first years: "When I came home, we didn't have any money. We had to live in a government housing project. We paid $31 in rent. The first year in business we had a total income of less than $300." But there were other problems, too.

## TAKING A STAND AGAINST RACISM

In 1954, Georgia, along with other states in the South, was experiencing a period of immense social turmoil. The civil rights movement was gaining momentum, and racial tensions were brewing, particularly after the Supreme Court had ruled (in *Brown vs. Board of Education of Topeka*) that segregation in public schools and other facilities was unconstitutional. Across the South, thousands of white men were joining organizations that rejected the court's decision and supported segregation. One such group, the White Citizens Council, started a branch in Plains in 1955. The council claimed to "protect the rights of whites" and openly opposed court-ordered desegregation. Plains citizens wanted Carter to join, but he refused. At the time, he and Rosalynn's views on race were considered extremely liberal, and Miss Lillian was very outspoken about the issue as well. As some of their neighbors heard about the Carters' refusal to join, they boycotted the family business. The boycott only lasted a few weeks, but the Carters' operation still suffered. "I almost decided to leave and go back and work in the nuclear submarine business," Carter wrote. "But only because

In the 1950s, racial prejudice in the South was reaching a climax, as seen here in this 1956 photograph of white protesters in Fort Worth, Texas. Jimmy Carter and his family fought against discrimination against blacks, which at the time made the Carters unpopular and hurt their business.

of the substantiality of my family . . . [did] we survived that crisis, and there was a change that slowly took place in Southwest Georgia that made our racial attitudes more acceptable."

Financial success eventually arrived. Thanks to some of Carter's prudent decisions, including buying some new land and more warehouses, and acquiring a cotton gin, the business started to thrive. By the 1960s, the Carter farm had grown into a large operation, and Carter Warehouses became one of Georgia's biggest peanut wholesalers. By the time Carter ran for president, he owned or leased more than 3,100 acres of land and had a net worth of $600,000.

## CARTER IS INTRODUCED TO POLITICS

As Carter was establishing a reputation for being an upstanding businessman and successful farmer, he was also becoming more civic-minded and active in the church and community. He chaired the county hospital authority, served on the library board, and was president of the Plains Development Corporation and the Crop Improvement Association. And, like his father before him, he became a deacon for the Plains Baptist Church, and he taught Sunday school.

While he was serving on the church board, he once again found his racial views in conflict with those of his neighbors. In 1965 several church members wanted to ban blacks from Sunday services (they would only be allowed to attend funerals). Carter urged his fellow churchgoers to defeat the measure, but his family and a single other member were the only people to vote against the ban. The ban was passed, and, as a result, he resigned his post as deacon.

Carter also served on the Sumter County Board of Education from 1955 to 1962, chairing it from 1960 to 1962. When he backed a plan that would consolidate some schools, many people thought that he and others were really just trying to integrate them. The plan was therefore defeated. Despite this setback, Carter was becoming more impassioned about his views, and he was doing more thinking about himself and his role in relationship to his fellow citizens.

When a new senatorial seat (the 14th district) was created in 1962, Carter's friends suggested that he run for office. Although he wasn't interested at first, Carter soon changed his mind. His business was doing well, and he felt ready for a change. Because of his experience on the school board, he had intimate knowledge of the school system, so he decided to run "just to protect the public school systems," he wrote. Carter announced his candidacy on September 30, and he campaigned hard to win the seat that would represent seven counties.

Carter's first foray into politics quickly showed him how dirty and corrupt that world can be. Initially, Jimmy Carter was thought to have lost the primary election by 139 votes. But a campaign worker named Joe Hurst had been observed intimidating voters at the Quitman County polls. He had approached voters, put his arm around them, and pressured them into voting for Carter's opponent, a hardware store owner named Homer Moore. Hurst had even stuffed ballots with votes from dead people and people in prison. Carter, who wrote that he was "mad as hell," challenged the election results. There was a new count, and three days before the general election Carter was declared the winner of the primary. He then beat his Republican opponent by around one thousand votes, and began his term in January of 1963.

As a senator, Carter served two consecutive two-year terms, and he established a reputation for being fiscally conservative (much like his father) and socially progressive (like his mother). Carter worked hard to cut back on governmental waste and eliminate some of the cushy benefits enjoyed by politicians. He also continued to be very interested in improving education. And he worked to repeal laws designed to discourage African Americans from voting.

## THE ROAD TO THE GOVERNORSHIP OF GEORGIA

In 1966 Carter decided to campaign for governor, but he entered the race late and lacked the adequate financial support to conduct a legitimate campaign. He also ran against an opponent whose name voters already knew. Lester Maddox was a restaurateur and an outspoken and avowed segregationist. Maddox's aggressively segregationist platform appealed to the many rural, conservative whites who found Carter's views on racial equality too liberal.

After Carter suffered a humiliating defeat in the election, he experienced a major crisis in faith.

"Maddox was a racist whose symbol was a pick handle that

Lester Maddox was Carter's rival for the governor's seat in Georgia in 1966. Maddox, a conservative who was against rights for blacks, was almost the exact opposite of Carter, whose liberal leanings were unpopular in the South at the time and led to his initial defeat.

he used to beat African Americans over the head if they tried to come in his restaurant," Carter said. "And when the returns came in, Maddox had been elected governor. And I basically renounced my faith. I felt that God had turned against me." His sister Ruth Carter Stapleton, a noted evangelist, helped him through his feelings of anger and disappointment. He became "born again" and dedicated his life to Jesus Christ. Ruth encouraged him to forget about politics for a while and do something different, and that's when Carter traveled around Georgia, encouraging people to change their lives through Christianity. "Out of that, my faith was strengthened," he said.

Then he got back to work, focusing like a laser beam on the next election. "I did not intend to lose again," he recalled.

From 1966 to 1970, the Carters were extremely busy, concentrating most of their energies on winning the campaign. The birth of their last child, Amy Lynn, on October 19, 1967, also energized them with a sense of purpose. Rosalynn and her husband traveled all over the state. Carter made some 1,800 speeches, and he seemed to make a point of appealing to the conservative, rural, working people who had voted against him in the previous election. He adopted the peanut as the symbol of his campaign, as he thought that it represented the values he stood for: hard work and simplicity. But Carter also made some moves in this campaign that his critics believe were hypocritical. He said that he was against busing black students to achieve integration in the schools, and he also painted his heavily favored opponent, former governor Carl Sanders, as a liberal. Plus he refused to condemn the notorious segregationist Alabama governor George Wallace. Although Carter was viewed as a dark horse, his campaign tactics worked. He beat Sanders in the 1970 primary, and he went on to win the November general election, gaining 60% of the votes and defeating Hal Suit, the Republican opponent.

## CARTER IMAGINES A "NEW SOUTH"

Jimmy Carter was sworn in as Georgia's 76th governor on January 12, 1971. His inaugural address shocked many Georgians, including his constituents and campaign workers, when he called for an end to racial discrimination. He said, "No poor, rural, weak, or black person shall ever have to bear the additional burden of being deprived of the opportunity of an education, a job, or simple justice. The time for racial discrimination is over." This declaration brought him national attention, and he received much press. No other Georgia governor had even come close to uttering such a statement about racial equality. Carter encapsulated what was

Despite his initial loss, Carter won a second bid to become the governor of Georgia in 1970. He served as governor until 1975.

being called the "New South." It was a new, more moderate South, a South that was slowly moving away from the racism and discrimination that had pervaded it for so long.

Carter entered the governor's mansion and immediately set to work on the things that mattered most to him, such as governmental efficiency. He wanted to streamline the way the state had been run. He assembled teams that closely analyzed how each state agency worked. Using the information that his teams gleaned from their research, Carter consolidated three hundred offices, agencies, and commissions into under 30 brand-new agencies. He also introduced zero-based budgeting, a procedure that required every governmental official to justify every budgetary request.

Carter also set about creating more opportunities for African Americans in government. He appointed blacks to state agencies and boards. The number of African American state employees rose by about 40% while Carter was governor. In 1974, he decided to hang a portrait of civil rights leader Martin Luther King Jr. in the state capitol. He also hung pictures of two other African Americans (Bishop Henry Turner and Lucy Laney) who played pivotal roles in Georgia's history. These gestures were controversial, to say the least. They prompted the racist KKK to organize a protest outside the building, and Lester Maddox vowed that he would become governor and remove the portraits.

Under Carter's leadership, the state passed a law that cut down on secrecy in government—the "sunshine law" allowed the public to attend governmental meetings. He pushed through a law that would provide an equal amount of financial aid to schools in wealthy and poor areas. He worked to reform the prison system, and started community centers for developmentally disabled children. But he also fought for stricter sentences for drug offenders. Additionally, Carter created a Civil Disorder Unit. Three state patrol officers, in plain clothes, would mediate between opposing sides when a racial clash seemed imminent. Viewed as highly successful, the program became a model for other states. This program was also one of the first manifestations of a theme that would run through Carter's public life—peacekeeping.

Before ecological conservation became a big issue in American politics, Carter recognized the importance of protecting precious wilderness areas and wild lands. As governor, he passed laws that added tracts of land to the state parks system, and he worked to preserve Georgia's wild rivers and historic sites.

Governor Carter was selected by his fellow governors to

serve as chair of the Southern Regional Education Board, the Appalachian Regional Commission, and Southern Growth Policies Board. He was very active in the national Democratic party, heading the 1972 Democratic Governor's Campaign, which worked on getting Democratic governors elected, and chairing the Democratic National Campaign Committee in 1974.

In the middle of Carter's term as governor, he noticed that there didn't appear to be a strong Democratic candidate for the presidency. Although he was still not well known, he thought that he could bring freshness and integrity to the presidency. He believed that his "outsider" qualities (peanut farmer, churchgoing man of integrity) could work in his favor. And Georgia state law said that he couldn't be governor for two consecutive terms. He saw an opening, and in January of 1975, Carter announced his candidacy for the 1976 Democratic presidential nomination.

Carter's grass-roots presidential campaign was an almost unprecedented success story. In the span of just a few months, he rose from a little-known governor to a national political force. In this photograph, Carter speaks at the Illinois Democratic Convention in Chicago on September 10, 1976.

# 5

# Politics and the Road to the Presidency

When the one-term governor from Georgia first announced his candidacy for the presidency in 1975, most people were completely surprised—even Jimmy Carter's mother! When she heard that he would be running for president, Miss Lillian famously asked, "President of what?"

Indeed, the idea that a peanut farmer from Plains would become president of the United States of America seemed a preposterous notion at the time. After all, not since Andrew Johnson one hundred years earlier had a man raised in the South gone on to occupy the highest office in the land. And Carter had never been a national candidate, had no significant experience with national politics, and claimed no close ties to the Washington world. But his tireless, methodical hard work and down-home charm would prove the skeptics wrong. In fact,

Carter's successful campaign is a paradigm of what could happen when focused determination meets good sense. His rise from obscurity to the Oval Office was nothing short of meteoric.

When Carter gathered together his family and announced his candidacy in January of 1975, it barely registered on the national radar. The press and the public hardly noticed, and even his friends were apprehensive. But that soon changed. Like he had done with so many previous challenges, Carter dedicated himself to doing everything possible to secure the nomination. Recognizing that much of the country had prejudicial ideas about Southerners, he took speech classes to reduce his drawl. He read as many newspapers and magazines as possible, and he kept highly informed about public affairs in the national and foreign spheres. He read several books a week and studied up on economics, national defense, and international relations. Carter pored over information about energy conservation and nuclear disarmament, issues critical to contemporary Americans. "The most important purpose of all was for me to learn this nation— what it is and what it ought to be," Carter wrote. He was developing a specific campaign strategy and some ideas about what he thought the country needed at the time.

## THE WHITE HOUSE BECOMES RIPE FOR A CHANGE

In 1975 the United States was still reeling from the effects of the Watergate scandal. In 1972 members of President Richard Nixon's reelection committee had attempted to break into and burglarize the Democratic Party's National Headquarters in the Watergate building. After Nixon's advisers tried to illegally cover up the debacle, the president himself was ultimately implicated, and he resigned. When Vice President Gerald Ford took over the Oval Office, he pardoned Nixon for his role in the scandal, but the American people were still understandably disillusioned

The years before Carter's election were rocked by political scandal, such as President Richard Nixon's (pictured here) involvement in the Watergate affair, in which he was implicated in the attempted burglary of documents from the Democratic Party's national headquarters. Gerald Ford, Carter's opponent in the election, had been Nixon's vice president, and his association with Nixon's tarnished image would work in Carter's favor.

with Washington and its politics. Also, a dark pall remained in Washington and the country following United States involvement in the Vietnam War.

Carter sensed that his lack of national experience and

"outsider" status might work to his advantage under these conditions. He was completely removed from the Watergate scandal. He also was a religious man with deep moral convictions, and he had a squeaky-clean image. Carter knew that he could be perceived as the antithesis of the corrupt Washington politician. Americans needed to trust government again, and he felt that he could be the one to restore decency and dignity back to the American presidency.

There were other factors that Carter was considering, too. For various reasons, the Democratic Party had been highly fragmented in recent years. Since 1964 most conservative Southern Democrats had voted for Republican candidates. These Democrats didn't agree with what they perceived as the liberal platform of the majority of the party—"liberalism" had become a dirty word to many people. Most of the other Democrat contenders for the presidency were viewed as liberal (George Wallace was the only conservative Democrat, and he was *extremely* conservative), so Jimmy thought that if he positioned himself as a moderate, he would appeal to different types of Democrats, including the conservative ones.

He recognized that much of his background reflected the same solid, core values that those voters held: he was Christian, he was a hardworking farmer, and he had a military background. He believed he could bring Southerners back to the party, while still attracting liberal voters, thereby unifying the Democratic Party.

With all this in mind, Carter immediately got to work, campaigning almost full time after leaving his office as governor. He had a lot to do: raise funds, talk to people and hear their concerns, and organize a nationwide group of volunteers that would believe in him and work hard for him. He took advantage of the connections he had made during his terms as head of the 1972 Democratic Governors Campaign Committee, and as chair of the 1974 Democratic

Campaign Committee. Although his work for these committees helped to assemble a broader constituency outside of his home state, in early 1975 he was still largely unknown to the American public.

## THE GRASS-ROOTS CAMPAIGN

In the beginning of his campaign, Carter traveled across the country and spoke to people about his ideas, but often he ended up addressing empty halls. At one press conference in Philadelphia, for example, just two people showed up—Carter and his press secretary. But Carter persevered, working ever more diligently and gradually building up a base of supporters and assembling volunteers. He talked about government reorganization, energy conservation, health care, welfare, and improving the struggling economy. In all, he campaigned outside of Georgia for about 250 days in 1975. "While the others have been building a money base," he declared at the time, "we've been building a people base."

In October of that year, a public opinion poll ranked possible contenders for the Democratic presidential nominee, and Carter's name wasn't even on the list. But in January of 1976 everything started to change. Because Carter needed to gain visibility and prove himself, he decided to enter most of the 31 Presidential Primaries. At the Iowa Caucus, the first contest to elect delegates to the '76 Democratic National Convention, Carter performed very well. He received more votes than any other candidate. This early victory finally brought him national credibility as a candidate, and he started to receive more and more coverage in the media.

That same month, a close friend of Carter's, Hamilton Jordan, organized a loyal group of Georgians who so believed in their candidate that they were willing to travel far from their homes to campaign for him, using money from their own pockets. This devoted team was known as the "peanut brigade," and they proved invaluable to Carter's bid for the presidency. They began in New Hampshire, the site of the first significant primary election of 1976. They went canvassing door-to-door, meeting with people and talking about their friend Jimmy. They covered Nashua, Manchester, and other small towns, spreading their enthusiasm and dedication to the man who had previously been referred to as "Jimmy who?" The group intended to visit 25,000 households, with each volunteer contacting 55 households per day. They spoke about Carter's ideals and his vision for a more efficient, more compassionate government. The people of New Hampshire were impressed, and they admired Carter's honest, simple, straightforward approach. Here was a candidate, *finally,* who offered hope and inspiration. The man from Georgia had won over the citizens of New Hampshire, and he earned the most votes in the February primary. Now the whole country started paying Carter much more attention.

## CARTER RISES ABOVE THE COMPETITION

At that point in the campaign, there were ten other men seeking the Democratic nomination, including Carter's main opponents: Senator Henry Jackson of Washington, Governor George Wallace of Alabama, and Representative Morris K. Udall of Arizona. All three of them were much better known than Carter, and they had considerably larger power bases. But Carter's campaign was rapidly gaining momentum. When he was endorsed by Representative Andrew Young, an African-American from Atlanta who had been Martin Luther King Jr.'s closest aide, Carter won the support of the black community. And his strategy was working; his moderate stance was drawing the support of conservatives and liberals, and he was appealing to both the rich and the poor.

In March he defeated George Wallace in Florida, winning another crucial primary contest. Maine, Oklahoma, and Vermont followed—Carter won them all. In Wisconsin the peanut brigade again worked their magic, helping Carter to narrowly defeat Morris Udall. The polls revealed that Carter was becoming the top choice of Democrats for the presidential nomination. Other candidates soon dropped out of the race, and Carter gained the support of their delegates. He eventually went on to win 19 of 31 primaries, eliminating all other candidates. By June he had the 1,505 delegates needed to win the Democratic National Convention.

Carter now had to consider whom he would choose as his running mate. He interviewed various people, and eventually decided on Senator Walter F. Mondale from Minnesota. As a liberal from the northern part of the country, it was thought that Mondale's presence would balance out the Democratic ticket. Also, "Fritz" Mondale had a good record with labor unions, whose support Carter needed (the South was traditionally anti-organized labor).

In August of 1976, after Carter had covered 400,000 miles and delivered 2,000 speeches, he received the Democratic Party's nomination for president of the United States. When he accepted the nomination at the Democratic National Convention in New York City, he stood before the delegates and smiled broadly, warmly, and proudly. He said, "Hello, I'm Jimmy Carter, and I'm running for president of the United States." He addressed the cheering crowd, saying that it was a "time for healing." He promised that he would be more responsive to the American people. He also spoke about revitalizing the struggling economy by creating new jobs. Now Carter had to concentrate on defeating his Republican opponent, the incumbent president Gerald Ford, who had just been nominated at the Republic National Convention.

## FORD VERSUS CARTER

President Ford had several things working against him. First, and most important, he would always be associated with the troubled and corrupted Nixon administration. And his decision to pardon Nixon for his role in Watergate was perceived by Americans as misguided. Also, the American economy was in crisis during Ford's presidency: 8% of United States workers were unemployed. Additionally, President Ford was constantly portrayed as weak and bumbling by the media. For example, he had been caught on camera as he tripped while boarding *Air Force One*, and comedy shows relentlessly parodied him. Gerald Ford was having difficulty earning respect.

Both Ford and Carter played off the other's weaknesses. Ford depicted Jimmy Carter as an inexperienced liberal who would raise taxes, while Carter painted Ford as an extension of the disgraced Nixon. Carter blamed Ford for the nation's high unemployment rate and the sorry state of the economy, while Ford charged that Carter's economic plan to create new jobs by increasing federal spending would cause rapid inflation.

Carter had a lead in the polls, thanks largely to his homespun image and warm charm. In some polls, he was ahead by 30 percentage points. But Carter's persona was somewhat sullied after he was interviewed in *Playboy* magazine in September of 1976. In the article, Carter confessed that he had "felt lust in his heart" while he was married to Rosalynn. This pronouncement was very controversial, particularly since so much had been made of Carter's wholesomeness and strong moral convictions. Carter lost the support of some fundamentalist backers, and because of this incident and some other issues his lead over Ford started to shrink.

Ford, who selected Senator Robert Dole as his running mate, needed to persuade more citizens to vote for him, and

As a liberal Democrat, Carter aspired to reach out to people of all ethnic and economic backgrounds. He often gave speeches in historically underprivileged areas of the country, such as this campaign talk in New York's Harlem in October of 1976.

he thought that he could do this by debating Carter. Ford and his advisers felt that he would appear more "presidential" than Carter during a debate. Before election day, Carter and Ford debated on three separate occasions, and vice presidential candidates Dole and Mondale debated once. The first presidential

During the presidential campaign, incumbent Gerald Ford and challenger Carter debated three times face to face. This photograph was taken during their first debate, in Philadelphia in September of 1976.

debate took place in Philadelphia, on September 23, 1976, and it focused on domestic affairs and economic issues. Jimmy seemed tentative and nervous at first, but he soon regained his poise. The second debate, held in San Francisco on October 6, dealt with foreign policy. Carter debated well, and he was more comfortable and aggressive. But Ford's performance baffled almost everyone. He made a big mistake when he claimed that the Soviet Union was not dominating Eastern European countries at the time—this made him come across as extraordinarily naïve, and some people even questioned the state of his mind. The vice presidential debate occurred in

Houston on October 15. More people were impressed with Mondale than with Dole, and this helped the Democrats further. The last debate, held on October 22 in Williamsburg, Virginia, covered all issues. But neither candidate outperformed the other. This race was going to be too close to call.

Finally, on November 2, 1976, Jimmy Carter defeated Gerald Ford in the closest presidential election since 1960, when John F. Kennedy beat Richard Nixon. Carter won 51% of the popular vote, and he gained 297 electoral votes compared to Ford's 240. The American people had spoken, and Jimmy Carter became the 39th president of the United States.

President Jimmy Carter waves to a crowd in Atlanta, Georgia, on November 3, 1976, after hearing he has won the election. Next to him are his wife, Rosalynn, and their daughter, Amy Lynn.

# 6

# President Carter and Domestic Issues

On January 20, 1977, in front of the U.S. Capitol, James Earl Carter was sworn in as president of the United States of America. During his campaign, Carter had demonstrated an uncanny talent for sensing the changing moods of the American public and acting and reacting accordingly. He had indeed proved himself a skilled and capable campaigner, but the country and the world were curious to see what type of president he would make.

In his inaugural address, Carter spoke about restoring honesty and dignity to the presidency. President Carter had high hopes for the country: "Our nation can be strong abroad only if it is strong at home, and we know that the best way to enhance freedom in other lands is to demonstrate here that our democratic system is worthy of emulation." Among other things, he wanted to get rid of waste in government, cut back on military spending and eliminate nuclear weapons, establish a healthcare program, reform the educational system, protect the environment, and improve the struggling economy. There was much President Carter wanted to achieve.

But Carter became president at a very troubled time. The office of the presidency had lost a lot of respect because of the Watergate scandal; Congress was embittered; the Democratic Party itself was fragmented; and the economy was in shambles. Carter had many challenges ahead of him, and it was going to be a difficult voyage. But President Carter stuck to his principles throughout his term, and he accomplished many of the goals that he set for himself and his country.

## CARTER, THE INFORMAL PRESIDENT

From day one of his presidency, Carter was intent on showing the American people that he was a new kind of president. He wanted to establish himself as a "president of the people." During his swearing-in ceremony, he insisted on using his nickname "Jimmy," and not "James Earl." And he did something highly unusual that first day. Rather than taking the traditional 1.2-mile ride down Pennsylvania Avenue in a bulletproof limousine, Carter decided to get out and walk. When President Carter and his family emerged from the car, people cheered wildly. "I felt a simple walk would be a tangible indication of some reduction in the imperial status of the president and his family," Carter wrote. This gesture revealed his desire to tear down the wall that separated the public from the president.

This was one of many steps Carter took to get rid of "some of the trappings" of the office. He often dressed casually for TV appearances, wearing jeans and cardigan sweaters. He also spoke in a more informal manner than most other politicians did. He sold the presidential yacht. Additionally, Carter urged his cabinet officers to drive their own cars; he

After his election, Carter selected his Cabinet from friends and allies from Georgia, rather than insiders from Washington. Here he meets with Cabinet members on December 28, 1976, on St. Simons Island, Georgia. His Cabinet selection was typical of the new president's behavior as an "outsider" to the federal government, but neglecting Washington politicians would later prove to be a mistake.

put an end to the playing of "Hail to the Chief" at public appearances (though he eventually reinstated this custom when people thought there wasn't *enough* pageantry); and he reduced the size of the White House staff by a third.

In an effort to make the country more unified, President Carter had many press conferences. He also held town meetings in small communities in the country. When selecting his cabinet, he bypassed Washington insiders, and instead filled many posts with allies from Georgia. He named fellow Georgian Griffin Bell the Attorney General; Bert Lance, a banker from Atlanta, became the director of the Office on Budget and Management; Jody Powell became his press secretary; and Hamilton Jordan, the organizer of the "peanut brigade," was named a presidential assistant. But he also appointed many women and minorities to his Cabinet. Other significant (non-Georgian) players in Jimmy Carter's administration included: Secretary of State Cyrus Vance, Secretary of the Treasury Michael Blumenthal, and Secretary of Defense Harold Brown.

## THE CARTER FAMILY IN THE WHITE HOUSE

Rosalynn contributed much to the Carter administration. She had been her husband's invaluable partner for years, and she continued in that role at the White House. Rosalynn was invited to cabinet meetings, and she was briefed on many issues. She also had her own chief of staff. She even served as an emissary to Latin America in 1977. She promoted women's equal rights, worked for the improvement of care for the elderly, advocated for children's immunizations, and was honorary chairperson of the President's Commission on Mental Health. Rosalynn also promoted the arts, arranging many performances of American and international artists at the White House.

Miss Lillian was a much-loved member of the first family. Americans admired her independence and moxie. They respected the energetic woman who had become a Peace Corp volunteer in India when she was 68. She was known as the "First Mother of the World." Amy Carter, the president's youngest child and the only one who grew up in the White House, was nine years old when her father became president. She attended public schools in Washington. The Carters tried to keep her out of the public spotlight, though that wasn't always possible.

But the Carter family member who seemed to attract the lion's share of the public's attention was Jimmy's brother, Billy. The former gas station owner, who also sold mobile homes, became a minor celebrity when Carter moved into the Oval Office. He had a reputation for being a hard drinker, even going so far as to have a beer named after him—Billy Beer. And his reputation was further tarnished— along with that of his brother, the president—when he accepted money to lobby for the Libyan leader and terrorist Muammar al-Quaddafi.

## MAKING CHANGES

Carter's first few months in office in 1977 seemed to go well, and the polls reflected as much. He had followed through on some of his promises and was working hard at achieving many more of them. One of his first official actions as president was the pardon of Vietnam-era draft evaders. He had made the controversial pledge during his campaign, and he kept his promise, issuing the pardon on January 21.

In March, Congress ratified his request for the authority to consolidate federal agencies and bureaus. Carter wanted to do the same thing in the White House that he had done when he was governor of Georgia—namely, get rid of too much bureaucracy and eliminate agencies that were unnecessary. In August of that year, Congress passed legislation that established a new executive department: the Department of Energy. Carter appointed James Schlesinger, formerly President Nixon's secretary of defense, to head the new department.

In June, Carter's legislation to halt the manufacture of B-1 (manned) bombers was passed. This was another issue that he had spoken about while campaigning. Carter thought that the program to produce the weapons was far too expensive. (The cost was estimated to be about $25 billion.) He instead promoted the development of the cruise missile—a missile that can be launched from submarines and airplanes and targeted to avoid enemy defenses.

Although Carter submitted many other proposals to Congress throughout his presidency, he was unable to push most of them through. He made a grave error when he neglected to establish a solid, working relationship with leaders in Congress, even though both the Senate and the House of Representatives had Democratic majorities. His status as an "outsider" helped him get elected, yet his lack of experience and connections in Washington politics terribly hindered him once in office. He seemed to ignore his own party's congressional leaders, particularly Speaker of the House Tip O'Neill, whose backing was crucial. Throughout his term, he was never able to rally the support he desperately needed for big programs and ideas. This was one of Carter's biggest failings as president.

But Carter remained committed to his goals throughout his years in office, and he did find some success with certain initiatives. Education had been a priority for him since he was on the Plains school board, and he continued to fight for quality education. In September of 1979, Congress established the Department of Education. He also increased financial aid for students by 25%, improved loan plans for college students, and doubled the budget for education.

Carter achieved some successes with environmentalism and conservation, too. He passed into legislation the Alaska Lands Bill, one of the most important environmental bills enacted in recent history. Ratified on December 2, 1980, the law set aside for preservation 104 million acres of wild Alaskan land. This single act more than doubled the size of America's national parks and wildlife refuges, and it virtually tripled the amount of U.S. land designated as wilderness area. Carter also developed the Superfund project, which was signed into legislation on December 11, 1980. The Superfund, overseen by the Environmental Protection Agency (EPA), investigates sites around the nation where chemical waste has been dumped. If Superfund workers find the site to be toxic and dangerous, it is their responsibility to see that it is cleaned up. Other accomplishments included the deregulation of the trucking, railroad, and airline industries. This action worked to stimulate competition

Among his achievements as president was Carter's success in preserving American wilderness. On December 2, 1980, just before leaving office, he signed a bill that protected 104 million acres of land in Alaska, doubling the area of America's national parks and wildlife refuges.

and lower fares. Additionally, Carter improved the Civil Service system.

But President Carter could not get congressional support on changes in immigration policy, new election funding procedures, a plan to eliminate the Electoral College, and many other initiatives. And some of the projects he most cared about, such as a national health insurance program or proposals for welfare reform, never received enough backing to get anywhere.

## CARTER BATTLES THE ENERGY CRISIS

The biggest domestic problems of Carter's presidency were the state of the economy and the energy crisis. He had criticized President Ford for not bringing down the inflation rate, yet during Carter's presidency the situation was getting worse. Inflation rose to 4.8% in 1976; 6.8% in 1977; 9% in 1978; 11% in 1979; and around 12% in 1980. The unemployment rate was also still very high. But the economic mess was not entirely within Carter's control. Between 1973 and 1980 inflation had climbed steadily. This was largely the result of the United States' increasing dependence on foreign oil. The country was using much more oil than it was producing.

In the early 1970s, Arab OPEC (Organization of Petroleum Exporting Countries) nations put an embargo on oil supplies to the United States. They did this to pressure U.S.-supported Israel to return the Arab land it had gained during the 1967 Six-Day War. The embargo caused inflation rates to soar. When OPEC lifted the embargo in 1974, U.S. suppliers of oil and natural gas were running out of fuel. Because the OPEC countries could charge whatever they wanted, oil prices increased substantially. When Jimmy Carter took office, the price of gasoline went from forty cents a gallon to more than seventy cents a gallon.

The high oil prices triggered even higher inflation rates. This, in turn, caused high interest rates and more unemployment, particularly in industrial cities such as Pittsburgh and Detroit. And the federal deficit was also in bad shape. Carter had promised to wipe out the deficit, but it had grown worse in 1977—to $66 billion.

By 1978, Carter's popularity had plummeted. The economy was struggling, and he was not connecting well with Congress. Additionally, there was an embarrassing scandal involving his good friend Budget Director Bert Lance. Lance had been accused of illegal activities while he was president of a Georgia bank. This was particularly scandalous because Jimmy Carter had talked so much about honesty and decency in government. Although the trial dragged on for months, causing Lance to resign from office, he was eventually cleared of the charges. But the issue hurt Carter's administration, and it was a distraction that took his attention away from the nation's more pressing matters.

Carter had myriad problems to deal with, but he was doing his best to tackle them. The president put forth a proposal to address the energy crisis. He urged Americans to cut back on their energy use, and he warned that domestic supplies of petroleum and natural gas were almost depleted. His package aimed to stimulate the economy by increasing production and cutting back on oil consumption. But Congress, once again, didn't support the program, and Carter was unable to implement his energy initiative. However, they did ultimately approve of a simplified version. This plan called for a reduction in U.S. oil imports. It also asked Americans to drive fuel-efficient cars; owners of cars that used excessive amounts of gas were penalized. Carter further pressed for the research and development of alternative energy sources, such as solar, nuclear, and geothermal power. But the economy wasn't improving, and inflation rates continued to climb.

By the spring of 1979, OPEC had slashed oil production, and the Iranian revolution that was occurring at the time contributed to a further increase in oil prices. The situation in the United States was becoming still more dire. Americans waited for hours at the gas pumps, and on the weekend of July 4, 1979, almost half the gas stations in many states had to close down because there was no gas to sell. Approximately 90% of all gas stations in the New York area shut down, and 80% closed in Pennsylvania. Carter's approval rating was sinking lower and lower. Americans viewed him as ineffectual, weak, and unable

The energy crisis of the 1970s was a serious problem for the Carter administration. Seen here are members of OPEC (the Organization of Petroleum Exporting Countries) attending a conference in Abu Dhabi, the capital city of the United Arab Emirates. The Arab countries that made up OPEC pressured the United States to stop supporting Israel by limiting the amount of exported oil. Although Carter tried to ease the problem with his new energy policies, his inability to resolve the crisis was a factor in his defeat in the election of 1980.

to lead the country. Carter realized that Americans were angry and tired of the hours-long gas lines. He decided to consult experts on how best to handle the situation.

After meeting with politicians, religious leaders, and

psychiatrists at his presidential retreat in Camp David, Jimmy delivered a speech on July 15 that addressed "the crisis of confidence that strikes at the very heart of our national will." He spoke more about developing alternative energy sources, higher taxes, and more stringent standards for fuel efficiency. The press and the public seemed to like this speech, which is why everyone was shocked when Carter asked for the resignations of most of his Cabinet soon after.

He made six changes to his Cabinet, and his close friend Hamilton Jordan became his White House Chief of Staff. Although Carter was trying to bolster his administration, many people thought that he was blaming his staff for his own failings. And now his speech appeared to be somewhat self-pitying and desperate. President Carter's popularity sunk even more.

In 1980, Carter introduced some more inflation-fighting programs, but the economy never improved throughout his presidency. By July of that year, Americans had become extremely frustrated. The economy was still ailing, and they were humiliated by the Iranian hostage crisis in which Iranians had captured 52 Americans. Americans seemed to have no faith in their president. That month, Carter's approval rating was at 21%, the lowest rating on record for any president. It was even lower than Richard Nixon's after the Watergate scandal.

Carter had entered the Oval Office with ambitious ideas for social, administrative, and economic reform in the United States. While he did achieve some successes, ultimately the horrendous state of the economy and the communication breakdown with Congress hampered his ability to be truly effective in the domestic front.

One of Carter's achievements in foreign policy was the signing
of two Panama Canal Treaties (Carter is seen here shaking hands
with the president of Panama). The treaty gave Panama control of
the important canal in 1999. While signing the treaty likely eased
political tensions in the area, many Americans saw it as a betrayal
that would weaken the United States' power overseas.

CHAPTER

# 7

# President Carter and International Affairs

W hen Jimmy Carter took office in 1977, many Americans were uncertain about what their role should be in the international arena. The Vietnam conflict had left them leery and ambivalent about American intervention abroad. Whereas past administrations had focused on preserving democracy and battling communism overseas, Carter wanted to concentrate instead on something that was especially important to him: human rights. In keeping with his desire to make the presidency more positive, he pledged to put support of human rights causes at the top of his foreign policy agenda.

Almost immediately, Carter made good on his promise. On February 24, 1977, Secretary of State Cyrus Vance announced that the United States would be reducing foreign aid to three nations because of their human rights violations. "I officially designated every U.S. ambassador on earth to be my personal human rights representative," Carter said, "and every embassy to be a haven for people who suffered from abuses by their own government. And every time a foreign leader met with me, they knew that human rights in their country would be on the agenda." While his human rights platform won him the respect of a large part of the international community, Carter's biggest foreign policy successes were to be found in his roles as negotiator and diplomat.

## THE PANAMA CANAL TREATIES

One of Carter's most significant accomplishments in the realm of diplomacy was achieved in 1978, when the Senate passed two treaties concerning the Panama Canal in Central America. The United States had controlled the canal since it was built in the early 1900s, but over the years many Panamanians resented U.S. ownership. The countries had been debating for years about the proper way to govern the canal, yet no conclusion had been reached. Carter thought that he could find a fair way to solve the problem.

The French first began construction of the Panama Canal in 1891, but financial issues and disease (many workers died of malaria and yellow fever) prevented the workers from completing it. The United States, which had been influential in Panamanian affairs since the mid-19th century, took over the project. After ten years of labor, the canal was built and functioning by 1914. The 51-mile canal, which enables ships to sail from the Atlantic to the Pacific Oceans, served as a highly convenient route for U.S. battleships and trading vessels.

Panamanians began to dislike the fact that there was an American presence in their nation, and the status of the canal became a major feature of Panamanian politics. In the 1950s Panamanian students demonstrated against U.S. control of the canal, and further rioting in 1964 led President Lyndon Johnson to begin negotiations with the Panamanian government.

President Nixon tried to continue discussions of the matter in 1971, but the Watergate incident interrupted the process. When Carter took office, he made a Panama Canal treaty a priority for his administration. Panamanians wanted sovereignty of the canal, and Carter thought that there might be rebellion in Panama if he didn't act. The president believed that a fair treaty was necessary, but it would have to be one that would allow both countries to share control of the canal.

After several meetings between United States and Panamanian representatives led by President Omar Torrijos, Carter achieved success. President Torrijos agreed to sign two treaties. One provided for the gradual transfer of the canal's operation to Panama by December 31, 1999. The other guaranteed that the canal would remain neutral in times of peace and war.

Now Carter needed to persuade Congress to ratify the agreements. Otherwise, the treaties would be meaningless. The president had to contend with lots of opposition from Republicans, and many Americans didn't approve of a treaty either. Some senators traveled to Panama to meet with General Torrijos and discuss the future of democracy in his country. But conservative Republicans were very reluctant to hand over control of the canal; they viewed the Panama Canal as a symbol of the United States' triumphant past. They thought that Carter betrayed vital American interests when he agreed to transfer control of the narrow strip. Gradually, President Carter started to gain some support. On April 18, 1978, both treaties were ratified, passing into legislation by a single Senate vote.

These negotiations represented one of the first times in Carter's presidency that he was able to showcase his sharp diplomatic skills. This was also the time when Carter began to develop a reputation as a hands-on president. Some critics thought he was *too* involved, however. They felt he was a micro-manager who was overly concerned with details. Carter played a part in almost every little aspect of the negotiations.

He even went so far as to meet with news anchorman Walter Cronkite to ensure that he pronounced Omar Torrijos's name correctly.

## ESTABLISHING RELATIONS WITH CHINA

Another milestone in Carter's presidency was his full diplomatic recognition of the People's Republic of China, a Communist-governed nation. In 1972, President Richard Nixon had courageously visited mainland China. This trip was significant in that it marked a new era in United States–Chinese relations. Carter's diplomacy continued the work that Nixon had begun.

After World War II, civil war raged through China, with the United States backing the nationalists and the Soviet Union supporting the Communists. In 1949, the Communists succeeded in their revolution, and the People's Republic of China was established. Meanwhile, the nationalist government was driven from the mainland to Taiwan, an island off China's coast. By 1971 China had become a major world power, with a seat on the United Nations Security Council and nuclear capability. The United States recognized that it was in the country's best interest to establish some relationship with the Communist regime. Richard Nixon, with his historic visit in 1972, took the first step. But after Nixon's trip, four years had gone by without any further movement toward formal recognition of the Communist People's Republic of China.

Carter first opened up Chinese–American relations by creating an arts exchange program. Then, on December 13, 1978, he sent his liaison, Leonard Woodcock, to meet with Vice Premier Deng Xiaoping and propose an expansion of relations between the nations. Deng received Carter's ideas favorably, and on December 15 the leaders sent an announcement to other heads of state around the world. The normalization of diplomatic relations between the United States and China was

His predecessor Richard Nixon had helped to open the door between China and the United States back in 1972, but it was President Carter who normalized diplomatic relations between the two countries, by speaking openly with Vice Premier Deng Xiaoping. This 1979 photograph, taken at a reception at the White House, shows Deng (right) with President Carter and Former President Nixon.

formalized in January of 1979. And later that month, Deng and his wife enjoyed a nine-day visit to the United States. Three of those days were spent with the Carters at the White House. This was the first ever visit to the United States by a senior Chinese Communist official. Former President Nixon was also present to receive Deng.

Although Carter won Congressional support for this agreement with China, the resumption of diplomatic relations with the nation was another thorny issue for the Carter administration. The official acknowledgment of the Communist government by the United States also signified the end of diplomatic ties with the nationalist Chinese government in Taiwan. The conservatives in Congress adamantly opposed recognition of any Communist government, and others were concerned that the United States would lose their trading relationship with Taiwan. But Taiwan and the United States continued to maintain economic and cultural ties through private organizations.

## NUCLEAR WEAPONS NEGOTIATIONS

Another initiative of Carter's was his work to eliminate nuclear weapons systems, an idea that had been part of his 1976 election platform. Nuclear disarmament was a highly controversial issue, both for people in the United States and abroad. Carter wanted to slow down the rapidly increasing supplies of nuclear weapons, but many politicians and Americans believed that the investment was necessary for their protection.

When World War II ended in 1945, the world had changed dramatically. It was separated into two new blocs of power. The Western bloc, which was capitalist and democratic, was led by the United States, while the Eastern bloc was headed by the Communist-ruled Soviet Union. The two superpowers spent the next four decades in tense opposition to one another in what became known as the "Cold War." During that period, both countries amassed an enormous amount of very powerful weapons. Americans and Soviets alike, and people in the rest of the world, were becoming more and more alarmed. The two nations started to amass enough nuclear weapons to destroy every living thing on the planet several times over.

In 1969 the United States and the Soviet Union began the Strategic Arms Limitation Talks (SALT), an attempt by both countries to limit the amount of weapons systems (mainly nuclear) in both countries. In 1972 both countries signed the SALT I Treaty, which restricted antiballistic weapons and offensive nuclear weapons. It also banned the building of new nuclear weapons systems for five years.

When Carter became president, SALT I had expired. Although the United States and the Soviets agreed to continue to adhere to the terms of that treaty, Carter got straight to work on preparing for SALT II. He worked closely with his staff, including Secretary of State Cyrus Vance, Secretary of Defense Harold Brown, National Security Advisor Zbigniew Brzezinski, and U.S. military leaders. Although Carter wanted to be on friendly terms with the Soviets so they could pass the second SALT treaty together, he was very concerned about the Soviet government's history of human rights abuses. Specifically, he wanted the Soviets to improve their treatment of dissidents. But again, Jimmy had to face more opposition in Congress. The conservatives were vigorously against SALT II. They claimed it would weaken the national defense and give the Russians an unfair advantage.

In June of 1979, Carter met Soviet President Leonid Brezhnev in Vienna, Austria. They spoke for four days. When Carter criticized the Soviets for their human rights record, they were angry. Brezhnev and his staff thought that the American president was interfering in their country's private affairs. But the leaders overcame this obstacle, and Carter and Brezhnev signed the Strategic Arms Limitation Treaty II on June 18, after five years of negotiations. "SALT II is the most detailed, far-reaching comprehensive treaty in the history of arms control . . . ," Carter said in a speech to Congress. "For the first time, it places equal ceilings on the strategic arsenals of both sides, ending a previous numerical imbalance in favor of the Soviet Union . . . but it's more

Nuclear-arms policy was also a priority in foreign relations during the Carter administration. The two nuclear superpowers, the United States and the Soviet Union, had amassed a huge arsenal of lethal weapons during the Cold War, and Carter, seen here with Soviet President Leonid Brezhnev, tried to negotiate the SALT II treaty to ease tensions. The U.S. Senate refused to ratify the treaty.

than a single arms control agreement. It is part of a long, historical process of gradually reducing the danger of nuclear war."

But SALT II would never win approval by the Senate, and it wasn't entirely the fault of conservatives in Congress.

In December of 1979, the Soviets invaded one of their neighboring countries, Afghanistan. Muslim rebels had toppled the pro-Communist government that had been backed by the Soviets. President Carter considered this a highly aggressive action. He stated, "An attempt by any outsider forces to gain control of the Persian Gulf region will be regarded as an assault on the vital interests of the United States of America, and such an assault will be repelled by the use of any means necessary, including military force."

Relations between the two countries deteriorated, and Carter took several initiatives, large and small, to protest the invasion. He postponed the opening of the new Soviet embassy in New York City and cancelled arts exchanges. The president then placed an embargo on the shipment of American grain to the Soviet Union, but this decrease on wheat sales to Russia somewhat backfired because it caused American farmers to lose money. And Carter boycotted the 1980 Olympic games in Moscow, the Soviet capital, to make his boldest statement against the invasion. He urged other countries to do the same. Finally, Carter asked the Senate to temporarily remove the SALT II treaty from consideration. "Our failure to ratify the SALT II treaty and to secure even more far-reaching agreements was the most profound disappointment of my presidency," he later said.

Though SALT II never passed into legislation, Carter had taken an important, necessary step in the movement toward Soviet and American nuclear disarmament. In the 1980s and 1990s, through a series of treaties, both countries started to disarm.

While Carter received praise for engineering the Panama Canal treaties, normalizing relations with China, and negotiating SALT II with the Soviets, his involvement in the Camp David Peace Accord is widely regarded as the high point of his administration.

By far the crowning achievement of Carter's foreign policy efforts was the Camp David Accord, in which a peace agreement was reached, thanks to Carter's diplomacy, between Egypt and Israel. Pictured, from left to right, are Israeli Prime Minister Menachem Begin, President Carter, and Egyptian President Anwar Sadat.

CHAPTER

# 8

# The Camp David Accord

**A**lthough many facets of Jimmy Carter's administration have been criticized, his role in what has come to be known as the Camp David Accord is universally viewed as his crowning achievement. Carter's brilliance was never more evident than when he brought together the leaders of two old enemies in the most significant moment of his presidency.

On August 5, 1978, Carter invited the president of Egypt, Anwar Sadat, and the prime minister of Israel, Menachem Begin, to Camp David, located in the Catoctin Mountains of Maryland. The official country residence of the U.S. president, Camp David is a quiet, private place that stretches over 143 acres of wooded land. Both leaders accepted immediately, hoping to end the 30 years of violence that existed between their two countries. The meetings began on September 5. Thirteen days later, the negotiators emerged with the framework for an historic agreement, a treaty that was a vital step in the movement toward peace in the war-torn Middle East.

Conflict has plagued the Middle East area since Biblical times. The region of Palestine, located on the eastern shore of the Mediterranean Sea, is considered sacred land by three different religious groups—Muslims, Jews, and Christians. It has been conquered and settled numerous times throughout history by both Jews and Arabs. Both groups consider this territory their rightful home.

After World War II (1939-1945), and Adolf Hitler's murder of millions of European Jews in the Holocaust, many people believed that an independent Jewish nation should be created. In 1948 the modern Jewish state of Israel declared its independence, causing much anger and resentment by the Palestinian Arabs, who were already living there. The new nation was surrounded entirely by Arab countries (Egypt, Syria, Jordan, and Lebanon) which had claimed the land as their own since early times. As Jews from all over the world moved to the new state, the Palestinian population and Arabs from neighboring countries attacked it. Violence has been a part of daily life in the region ever since.

As the wars raged on, hundreds of thousands of Palestinians left their homes and became refugees, staying in camps set up in neighboring countries. With the exception of Jordan, no Arab country would grant citizenship to the displaced people.

In the Six-Day War of 1967—in which Israel fought Egypt, Jordan, Syria, and Iraq—Israel expanded its land holdings to include the Golan Heights, the West Bank (of the Jordan River), the Gaza Strip, and the Sinai Peninsula. In the Arab-Israeli War of 1973, Arab nations attempted to win back the land, but they were not successful. In 1977 Egypt's president, Anwar Sadat, decided to try to end the strife between his country and its neighbor. Egypt had put a considerable amount of money into its military and weaponry, and as a

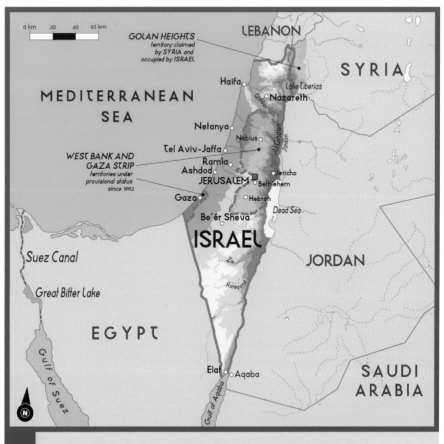

The creation of the state of Israel in 1948 resulted in wars, refugee camps, and enormous political tensions between Jews and Arabs in the Middle East. Carter studied the history of the region intensely in order to better understand each side's point of view, and this research undoubtedly helped him to negotiate the Camp David Accord.

result its economy was struggling; also, there was much social unrest. Sadat made a historic visit to Israel on November, hoping to open up communication, stop the military buildup, and seek some peace. The Israelis, led by Menachem Begin, greeted Sadat with enthusiasm. On Christmas day of that same year, Begin returned the gesture and visited Sadat in Egypt. The two countries started to make some progress in negotiations, but there were problems, and the talks came to an abrupt halt.

## CARTER SEEKS SOLUTIONS TO THE MIDDLE EAST CRISIS

While Begin and Sadat were trying unsuccessfully to end the suffering and bloodshed, Jimmy Carter was in Washington, immersed in reading about the Middle Eastern region and the history of the conflicts there. He was attempting to craft a plan for reconciliation. The president recognized that stability in the Middle Eastern region was important to the United States, and the entire world (for its strategic location and resources, primarily oil). Carter was also concerned that Egypt would turn to the Soviet Union for support, since the communist country had supplied the Egyptians with aid until Sadat became president in 1970. Carter consulted with Mondale, Vance, Brzezinski, Jordan, and other advisors, and hashed out his ideas with them. Then, on August 5, 1978, he contacted Begin and Sadat, inviting both of them, along with some of their staff, to Camp David. He thought that the quiet presidential retreat would be the perfect place to conduct the highly delicate negotiations.

The meetings started on September 5. Although the media knew, of course, about the summit, they were not given briefings of the day-to-day events. The leaders and their staff spent their days talking, debating, and negotiating about the complicated land-for-peace proposals. Sometimes the disagreements got so intense that Begin and Sadat refused to meet with each other. Carter handled the situation carefully, taking a step-by-step approach. He visited each of them separately, going back and forth between their cabins. (This was a variation of "shuttle diplomacy," a technique also practiced by Secretary of State Henry Kissinger during the early 1970s, when he flew back and forth between warring countries who refused to meet with one another.)

Carter and Sadat got along very well, and the president

admired Sadat's bravery and breadth of knowledge. He even considered Sadat a good friend. On the other hand, Carter found Begin to have a "stubborn streak." He also felt that Begin treated Sadat as his inferior. But President Carter insisted on treating both sides equally. Later, some people, including Carter's 1980 presidential election opponent, Ronald Reagan, who accused Carter of "cozying up" to the Arabs, believed that he was *too* open-minded. Carter lost the support of many American Jewish voters after the Camp David Accord was signed.

## THE CAMP DAVID ACCORD

However, it was (and still is) widely believed that Carter handled the very complicated negotiations masterfully, and that he proved himself to be a skilled mediator. The talks continued for 13 days, much longer than was originally anticipated. But on September 18, 1978, the leaders left Camp David and returned to Washington, where they announced that their deliberations had been successful. Next, they signed their agreement, two documents known as the Camp David Accord that provided the template for the formal peace treaty between Israel and Egypt that was to be signed in the next few months.

The first document, called the "Framework for Peace in the Middle East Agreed at Camp David," addressed the future of the Gaza Strip and the West Bank, and it dealt with the issue of the Palestinian peoples. The agreement was comprehensive and specific. It proposed a five-year transitional period in the West Bank and Gaza, when the Israel military government would gradually withdraw from the area. A fully autonomous Palestinian government, elected by the Palestinian residents of those territories, would be put in place. But Israeli forces would remain in specified sites to ensure Israel's safety. Additionally, no new Israeli settlements would be established in the area. The future settlements issue would be decided in talks among Egypt, Israel, Jordan, and the Palestinian inhabitants of the

(From left to right) Anwar Sadat, Jimmy Carter, and Menachem Begin sign the Camp David Accord at the White House in September of 1978.

West Bank and Gaza. Carter said during his address to Congress on September 18 that the agreement "outlines a process of change which is in keeping with Arab hopes, while also carefully respecting Israel's vital security."

The second document, called the "Framework for the Conclusion of a Peace Treaty Between Egypt and Israel," focused on the Sinai Peninsula and the relationship between Egypt and Israel. This document provided that Israel would return the Sinai Peninsula to Egypt between three and nine months after the signing of the formalized peace treaty. The agreement also called for several security zones, and foreign observers would be positioned in the Sinai to ensure that the treaty's provisions were being properly implemented. When the Israelis completed their withdrawal from the area, the two countries would establish full diplomatic recognition of one another. They would exchange ambassadors and treat each other as friends and good neighbors.

The official peace treaty was signed on March 26, 1979, in Washington. President Carter's peacekeeping skills won him admiration all over the world. His adept handling of the Camp David Accord was viewed very positively by the American public, as well, and his popularity increased markedly in the polls. He regained some of the respect that he had lost in the beginning of his administration. Although Anwar Sadat and Menachem Begin received the Nobel Peace Prize for their work on behalf of peace between their countries, many people felt that Jimmy Carter deserved it, too.

But the accords were not received well by other Arab leaders. They condemned the agreements, Egypt was expelled from the Arab League, and Carter's friend President Sadat was assassinated by extremists from his own country in 1981.

Carter, along with many others, recognized that the accord was only a first step. But it was a crucial, groundbreaking first step. He summed up the value of this event in his address to Congress on September 18: "For many years the Middle East has been a textbook for pessimism, a demonstration that diplomatic ingenuity was no match for intractable human conflicts. Today we are privileged to see the chance for one of the sometimes rare, bright moments in human history—a chance that we may offer the way to peace. We have a chance for peace because these two brave leaders found within themselves the willingness to work together to seek these lasting prospects for peace, which we all want so badly."

Carter's efforts to create peace in the Middle East were unpopular with militant Muslims, shown here protesting at the U.S. Embassy in Tehran, Iran, on November 8, 1979. A group of militants consequently stormed the embassy and took dozens of Americans hostage. This created a crisis that would effectively put an end to Carter's chances of re-election.

# 9

# The Iranian Hostage Crisis and the 1980 Election

In mid 1979, Jimmy Carter and his administration were confronting many challenges. The economy was still struggling, oil supplies were running out, and public morale was extremely low. But Americans had also just witnessed one of Carter's major successes—his signing of the historic Camp David Accord in March. However, this achievement and his other accomplishments were soon completely overshadowed by a major crisis that began in November of that year.

## THE HOSTAGE CRISIS BEGINS

On November 4, 1979, at 10:30 in the morning, a crowd of militant college students in Tehran, the capital of Iran, chanted "Death to America! Death to the Great Satan!" in front of the U.S. embassy. The angry mob had been gathering every day for the previous two weeks, but that morning they stormed into the U.S. embassy grounds. Helmeted U.S. Marines tried to repel them with tear gas, but the students forced their way in. The group then took 65 embassy staff members and American diplomats hostage.

The students immediately decided to set free the women and African-Americans, but they kept 52 Caucasian men, bound and blindfolded them, then paraded them in front of the crowd and TV cameras from around the world. This marked the beginning of one of the most humbling periods of American history. Americans, and the world, waited 444 long, frustrating days before the hostages were finally released.

Iranian resentment toward the United States had been intensifying for years. In 1953, the U.S. Central Intelligence Agency (CIA) assisted in restoring Iran's monarch, Shah Mohammad Reza Pahlavi, to the "Peacock Throne" of his ancestors. Iran has been one of the United States' major suppliers of oil. The shah was an important U.S. ally. His policies were pro-Western, and his presence in the Middle East helped protect U.S. interests. The United States supported the shah's regime for years. But he was a despotic tyrant. He and his family lived opulently while most Iranians languished in poverty. Although the shah had modern ideas, his regime was brutal. Iranian people lacked basic rights, and the shah's secular policies were enforced harshly by his American-trained secret police. Plus, his Westernized ideas alienated and offended the fundamentalist Muslims of his country.

In January of 1979, the Iranians revolted. After riots and demonstrations against the shah's rule, he was forced out of the country. Anti-American sentiment was rampant, and the revolutionaries threw their support behind Ayatollah Ruhollah Khomeini, the extremist Muslim religious leader who was then living in exile in France. In February, the

Ayatollah returned to Iran, declaring it an Islamic state.

Meanwhile, the shah was looking for a country that would allow him to stay. Egypt's president, Anwar Sadat, invited him to visit, and he also stayed in Morocco and Mexico. At that point, Carter's policy toward the deposed shah was reasonable: he wasn't allowed into the United States. Carter didn't want to ruin the possibility of establishing a relationship with the new Iranian government. But when, eight months later, the shah needed treatment for his cancer and gallstones, Carter took the advice of Henry Kissinger and other U.S. government officials. He granted the shah a visa to the United States for humanitarian reasons. On October 22, 1979, the deposed tyrant was admitted to New York Hospital–Cornell Medical Center.

This move infuriated the Iranians. A month later the revolutionaries seized the embassy in Teheran and took the hostages. The students demanded that the United States give up the shah to Iran, so the government could put him on trial. Only then, they said, would they release the hostages. The Iranian revolutionary government sanctioned the action. On November 4, the Iranian Foreign Ministry stated: "Today's move by a group of our compatriots is a natural reaction to U.S. indifference to the hurt feelings of the Iranian people about the presence of the deposed shah . . . in the United States. If the U.S. authorities respected the feelings of the Iranian people and understood the depth of the Iranian revolution, they should have at least not allowed the shah into the country."

President Carter immediately condemned the action, stating that it was a violation of international law. He insisted that the kidnappers release the 52 men, but they refused. He did his best to negotiate with them, wanting to avoid a direct confrontation with the Iranian government. But President Carter would not hand over the shah, claiming that the United States would not give in to blackmail.

A long standoff ensued between the two countries. Neither side budged.

## NEGOTIATIONS WITH THE IRANIANS PROVE UNSUCCESSFUL

Between November 9 and November 14, Carter, his cabinet, and his top advisers met daily to attempt to end the crisis. Many of President Carter's staff thought that this might mean war with Iran. But they were also concerned that the crisis would jeopardize Carter's 1980 presidential campaign. At one point, the national security adviser, Zbigniew Brzezinski, said: "Mr. President . . . It is important that we get our people back. But your greater responsibility is to protect the honor of our country and its interests. I hope we never have to choose between the hostages and our nation's honor, but . . . Mr. President, if they're still in captivity at Thanksgiving, what will that say about your presidency and America's image?" Cyrus Vance, the secretary of state, quickly retorted, "The hostages have been held only five days. We're dealing with a volatile, chaotic situation in Iran, and negotiation is the only way to free them."

Days passed, and as the weeks turned into a month, Carter was appearing more and more incompetent to the United States and the world. He was in a very sticky position. He was concerned about the safety and health of the hostages, so he didn't want to take any military action. And he was afraid that Iranian threats to punish, or worse, kill the American captives would be carried through. But succumbing to the Iranians' demands would make the American president and the whole nation look weak.

Months of negotiation yielded no results. The crisis dragged on. Americans, and television viewers all over the world, watched helplessly as mobs gathered in Tehran and chanted anti-American slogans and burned American flags. The nation felt utterly demoralized and humiliated. Many Americans were very unhappy with the way the president

There were many strategies that Carter employed to try to end the hostage crisis in Iran. Here, the president signs a document to freeze Iranian assets held in U.S. banks. This would prove ineffective, however, and the further failure of a rescue attempt that resulted in the death of eight American soldiers led Americans to see Carter as a weak leader.

dealt with the ordeal, and they pointed fingers at his administration for not having protected the diplomats and embassy staff in the first place.

Carter and his staff tried every reasonable approach to resolving the situation. He banned oil imports from Iran, expelled Iranian diplomats, froze Iranian assets of about

$13 billion, and cut off all trade between the two countries. Iran's president, Bani Sadr, began to get nervous and started to look for a way out of the situation. But Ayatollah Khomeini and other Muslim extremists shot down these attempts at negotiation.

On January 23, 1980, Carter said to the nation in his state of the union address: "Our position is clear. The United States will not yield to blackmail. We continue to pursue these specific goals: first, to protect the present and long-range interests of the United States; secondly, to preserve the lives of the hostages and to secure, as quickly as possible, their safe release, and if possible, to avoid bloodshed. . . . If the hostages are harmed, a severe price will be paid."

## THE HOSTAGE CRISIS HURTS CARTER'S CAMPAIGN

Meanwhile, Carter's approval ratings were dramatically declining. Nightly television news programs were keeping close track of every day that passed that the hostages spent in captivity. And Americans were also affected by letters from the hostages describing their conditions. In January, one of the captives, William Hode, wrote a letter to the *Washington Post*. He said, "We are being kept in semi-darkened rooms, our hands are tied day and night . . . because of the constant noise it is almost impossible to sleep."

Because Carter was doing so miserably in the polls, Senator Edward Kennedy from Massachusetts thought that he might have a good chance of defeating the president and winning the Democratic presidential nomination for the 1980 election. Throughout his term, Carter had serious conflicts with the more liberal and left-leaning Democrats like Kennedy. They thought he was too conservative on budgetary and defense issues, and they believed he wasn't truly committed to helping out the poor and minorities.

In August of 1979, the polls showed Kennedy leading Carter by a substantial margin. The American public thought that Carter's economic policies and domestic reforms had failed, and he was widely perceived as an ineffective leader. Inflation had climbed and unemployment remained high. Now the hostage crisis was looming ominously over everything else. But Carter chose not to campaign, opting instead to stay at home, in the White House, and devote his full attention to the crisis in Iran. He wanted to be available in case there were any developments in the hostage situation. He had been conducting some private negotiations, using Algeria, in North Africa, as a mediator. Although some ill hostages were released for humanitarian reasons, no other progress was made. The shah, in the meantime, left the United States for Panama, and then Egypt.

## A TRAGIC RESCUE ATTEMPT

On April 24, 1980, Carter made a decision that would have terrible consequences. Desperate, he approved a plan to send a military commando team to rescue the hostages. It was a mistake that would overshadow his successes in foreign policy and ultimately damage his presidential legacy. Six C-130 transport planes filled with 90 soldiers landed on a remote part of the Iranian desert. Eight helicopters were sent for the assault, but only six made it to the gathering site. The other two broke down while flying through an unexpected sandstorm. The operation was called off, but as the helicopters were withdrawing, one of them collided into a transport plane. Eight servicemen died in the fire that resulted from the crash, and four others were severely burned. The burnt bodies of the dead marines were put on display in the square of occupied embassy, bringing even more pain and frustration to the American public. The entire mission was a disaster, and Jimmy Carter seemed to have lost all credibility in the country and the world.

After this event, the hostages were moved to secret locations. Secretary of State Vance, who vehemently opposed the rescue attempt, resigned his position. Carter then named Senator Edmund Muskie as Vance's successor.

In June of 1980, the shah died while in Egypt. But Khomeini continued to hold the hostages to protest American policies toward Iran. He demanded the return of the shah's assets, the release of all Iranian assets in the United States, and a promise from the United States to keep out of Iranian affairs. The stalemate continued.

On August 2, Carter managed to earn the presidential nomination at the Democratic National Convention in New York. Although his approval ratings were low, he still received 2,129 votes to Kennedy's 1,146. During his acceptance speech, he highlighted his Camp David Accord and his achievements with his energy program. Meanwhile, the Republicans selected Ronald Reagan, the governor of California and former actor, as their presidential nominee. George Bush, the former U.S. ambassador to the United Nations, was Reagan's running mate.

When Carter received the presidential nomination, Ronald Reagan was way ahead of him in the opinion polls. After all, the hostages were still in Iran, the Russians continued fighting in Afghanistan (even after the Olympic boycott), and inflation and unemployment rates remained high. Republicans called Carter inept, and they said that his policies made the country weak. Reagan and Bush promised an economic turnaround, and Reagan's public charm, optimistic talk, and fierce belief in the greatness of his country seemed to cheer up a demoralized American public. On November 4, 1980, Ronald Reagan was elected president in a landslide victory. Reagan won 51% of the popular vote to Carter's 42%, but the electoral college gave 489 votes to Reagan and only 49 to Carter.

President Carter worked to secure the release of the hostages up until the very last days of his presidency. The Iranian government had started to show interest in ending the crisis when, on September 22, Iran went to war with its

Ronald Reagan, seen here with his wife, Nancy, waves to supporters at the Republican National Convention in 1980. After four years of low public morale under a presidency that was widely perceived to be weak, Reagan's optimistic message and superb speaking ability swept him into the White House.

neighbor Iraq. Khomeini then had to admit that he was unable to challenge two countries at once. The West German foreign minister, who was in Teheran, relayed to Carter that Khomeini was ready to discuss a resolution. After a few more months of talks, the president lifted the freeze on Iranian

On January 20, 1981, just minutes after Carter left the White House, Iran released the American hostages. One explanation was that Iran, which was now at war with neighbor Iraq, could not survive both the war and the economic pressure the United States was inflicting. Here, a jubilant Carter stands next to released hostage Bruce Laingen.

assets in the United States, and Khomeini agreed to release the men.

After being held in Iran for 444 days, the hostages were returned home on January 20, 1981, 35 minutes *after* Carter left office! Carter wasn't in Washington for Ronald Reagan's inauguration. Instead, he was on a plane, en route to the military hospital in West Germany where he would greet the freed hostages.

Since leaving office, Carter has been one of the most active former presidents in U.S. history. In this 2001 photograph, Carter helps to build a house in Seoul, South Korea, with his wife, Rosalynn. Carter has used his carpentry skills and leadership to make Habitat for Humanity, which builds homes for low-income families, a huge success.

# 10

# Citizen Carter: Peacekeeper and Humanitarian

When Jimmy Carter left the Oval Office on January 20, 1981, his work in public service wasn't over. In fact, in a way it was really just beginning. As Jimmy and Rosalynn Carter packed up their bags and headed back to Plains, they looked forward to spending some more time with each other and with the whole family. But, as Carter wrote, "I was not ready for retirement."

Since then, the former president has been quite busy. He has developed programs committed to fighting poverty and hunger in United States cities; he has traveled all around the globe, battling diseases, monitoring elections, building homes, immunizing babies, and preventing wars; he has received awards and countless praise for his work in support of human rights, conflict resolution, and social justice at home and abroad. While many people agree that Carter's presidency was troubled and flawed, his post-presidential record is generally acknowledged as unparalleled in American history. He could be the most highly regarded and admired ex-American president ever.

## CARTER THE AUTHOR

One of the ways Carter has kept busy is through his writing. He began his career as an author before he became president. After the barely known candidate won the New Hampshire Primary in 1976, his autobiography, *Why Not the Best* (1975), sold exceptionally well. But his life in letters went full steam ahead when he left the presidency. In addition to penning several political pieces for magazines, journals, and newspapers, he has published articles about some of his hobbies, including fly-fishing and carpentry. He has written several memoirs, including *Keeping Faith: Memoirs of a President* (1982), *An Hour before Daylight: Memories of a Rural Boyhood* (2001), and *Christmas in Plains* (2001). He published a book of poems called *Always a Reckoning* (1995). Other titles are *Living Faith* (1996), *Sources of Strength: Meditations on Scripture for a Living Faith* (1997), and *The Virtues of Aging* (1998). With Rosalynn, he co-wrote *Everything to Gain: Making the Most of the Rest of Your Life* (1987). He also wrote some books for children: *Talking Peace: A Vision for the Next Generation* (1993), and *The Little Baby Snoogle-Fleejer* (1995), which was illustrated by his daughter, Amy. Ten of his books have become *New York Times* bestsellers.

## HABITAT FOR HUMANITY

Many Americans most associate Jimmy Carter's ex-presidential life with his work for Habitat for Humanity. Jimmy, who has solid carpentry skills, and Rosalynn have both become regular volunteers for the Christian nonprofit organization, which builds homes for less fortunate people in the United States and all over world. Based in Americus, Georgia, about nine miles from Plains, Habitat for Humanity has become increasingly more popular since the Carters first got involved back in 1984. Now, one week every year, the Carters go to work for Habitat. With hammers in hand, they labor alongside other volunteers, including students, retired professionals, teachers, and other people from all walks of life. But the future homeowners get involved, too. They are required to work hundreds of hours on their homes, and on others for their neighbors. Organization officials say, "By investing themselves in the building process, homeowners gain self-reliance, self-esteem, and new skills . . . . Through the houses we build, hope is restored and lives are changed as the cycle of need is broken."

The organization accepts no state or federal funds; the building materials are either donated or paid for by the volunteers. Habitat for Humanity makes interest-free loans to the families so they can buy the homes.

The Carters' involvement with Habitat has taken them all over the country, from New York City to a Native American reservation in South Dakota. They have also built homes in Peru, Uruguay, and Nicaragua. But one project was particularly close to Carter's heart. In 1994, when the Flint River flooded, the home of 77-year-old Annie Mae Rhodes was destroyed. Annie Mae, of Albany, Georgia, had cleaned and cooked for Carter when he was a child. She was the Carter family house-keeper and cook for 22 years, and she was famous for her sweet potato pie and peanut bread. When a Red Cross worker told Carter about Annie Mae's troubles, he immediately got started on constructing a house for her and her sick brother. Although Annie Mae had arthritis, she pitched in and saw her new house to completion.

Carter wrote, "Habitat for Humanity is only one of many worthwhile programs in which anyone with a little time and inclination can perform challenging and useful work. There are so many people in trouble, so many needs right around us. We can fund programs to help the poor and the elderly, the hand-icapped, the imprisoned, the mentally ill, alcoholics, and drug addicts, to name a few. So many of our young people need a helping hand as do our hospitals, our libraries, art museums, and schools." Carter has worked hard to find ways to confront all of these problems, and he has accomplished a great deal, primarily through his foundation, the Carter Center.

In 1982 Carter became University Distinguished Professor at Emory University in Atlanta. With Emory, he established the Carter Center, which includes a presidential library and a museum. Unlike other ex-presidents, Carter wanted more than just a library built solely to hold historic documents and articles from his presidency. "I don't want a monument to me," Carter said.

## THE CARTER CENTER

One night after he left the White House, Carter had an idea. He woke up and said to Rosalynn, "I know what we can do at the library. We can develop a place to help people who want to resolve disputes. There is no place like that now. If two countries really want to work something out, they don't want to go to the United Nations and get 150 other countries involved in the argument. I know how difficult it is for them to approach each other publicly, and they take a chance on being embarrassed by a rebuff from the other party. We could get mediators that both sides would trust, and they could meet with no publicity, no fanfare, perhaps at times in total secrecy."

So the Center became something truly special: a place dedicated to promoting peace and democracy and supporting human rights all over the world. The Center provides a forum for discussion of national and international issues, but it's more than just a think tank. It is a place that actively gets things done. "All of our programs are—have to be—active in nature," said Carter. "We don't take a project just for scholarly analysis. . . . Unless we believe at the very beginning that there will be an action result, we don't take it on."

With the creation of the Carter Center, the former president established a unique forum in which nations could settle their disputes. As part of his work for the Center, Carter has traveled around the world as a political observer. Here he is shown in Monrovia, Liberia, where he watched over the Liberian presidential elections of 1997 to ensure fairness. Having an outside observer evaluate elections has helped third-world countries to affirm the legitimacy of their new governments.

The Carter Center has a staff of around 150 people. This includes scholars and other experts, in addition to several interns. It aims to provide health care and other services for the mentally ill; relieve poverty, hunger, and suffering; immunize babies; and fight disease and prevent sickness. The Center has had programs in Third World villages, urban American neighborhoods, and Native American reservations. The Center also sponsors lectures and discussions on both foreign and domestic issues. Through the Carter Center's Global 2000 program, Carter has also continued his work in environmentalism. This program focuses on improving health and agriculture in the developing world.

In 1991 Carter launched the Atlanta Project (also through the Carter Center), which brings together public and private efforts to solve social problems that affect families in inner cities. Some of the issues that the project tackles are unemployment, drug abuse, homelessness, and teenage pregnancy. Also in 1991, he founded the International Negotiation Network Council. Through this forum, former heads of state and other prominent leaders monitor elections and conduct negotiations for peace.

Since founding the Carter Center, Carter has responded to requests for his assistance all over the world. Members of his staff keep track of events in troubled areas and carefully examine the situations and people involved. If he is asked to monitor an election or mediate between hostile parties, his staff supplies him with all the information he needs. He reads about the country's culture and political history. He also studies the personal styles, values, and views of the leaders. (After years and years of practice, Carter understands that information-gathering is crucial to solving any problem.)

## AN INTERNATIONAL MAN OF PEACE

In May of 1989, Carter took a trip to Panama, where he and Gerald Ford led an international team of election observers. Using his facility with Spanish, Carter encouraged Panamanians to vote. When the team declared the results of the election fraudulent, Carter condemned Manuel Noriega's illegal practices. In February of 1990, Carter traveled to another Central American country, Nicaragua, a place he had been to the previous year to help broker an end to the long war between the Sandinistas and contra rebels. In Nicaragua he monitored an important election. When Daniel Ortega Saavedra lost, Carter advised him to accept his loss gracefully, thereby playing a critical role in the smooth transition to democracy.

Carter has also worked closely with election officials and voters in such countries as Haiti, Liberia, Jamaica, Mexico, Paraguay, the Dominican Republic, Mozambique, and Venezuela. In all, President Carter has overseen more than 20 elections overseas.

Carter's post-presidential pursuits are many and various, but it is his peacekeeping and diplomatic skills that garner him the most praise. In 1993 President Bill Clinton needed Carter's help in Somalia, a troubled African country. Carter opened up talks with the clan leader Mohammed Farah Aidid, and he helped prevent more U.S. military intervention.

In June of 1994, President Clinton requested Carter's assistance again. This time it was to resolve an unsettling international crisis with North Korea. The United States suspected that the country was developing powerful nuclear weapons. Eight thousand rods had been removed from a nuclear reactor, and the U.S. government was worried that the North Koreans would use the rods to create nuclear bombs. Their worries deepened when President Kim Il Sung refused to allow international inspectors into their plants. Some U.S. congressmen pushed to impose sanctions and others urged military action; but when Carter received a personal invitation from Kim Il Sung, he traveled to

Pyongyang to help ease the tension. After several days of negotiations, Carter—and everyone—was victorious. He left North Korea with an agreement detailing an end to their nuclear weapons program. Carter's negotiating skills were just as brilliant as they had been at Camp David. His initiative not only defused a potentially explosive (literally!) situation, it also paved the road to a historic treaty between two countries (North and South Korea) that ended 40 years of hostility.

In September of 1994, Carter once again came to President Clinton's rescue. President Clinton was on the verge of invading Haiti to oust a brutal, ruthless dictator. Carter instead persuaded Clinton to let him attempt peaceful negotiations. Carter and a team of others flew into Port-au-Prince, the Haitian capital, where U.S. warships were standing close by, ready to attack. He met with the leaders and masterfully facilitated their peaceful departure from the country. U.S. airplanes had already been in the air by the time Carter achieved his breakthrough. He managed to convince the dictator and his officers to transfer their power peacefully within a month and restore the democratic government of Jean-Bertrand Aristide.

In March of 1995, Rosalynn and Jimmy went to the African nation of Sudan. The war-torn nation (a civil war had been going on for 12 years at the time) was filled with people suffering from a disease caused by the Guinea worm. The illness had been killing millions of people each year in India and Africa, and Sudan had been hit especially hard. The Carters persuaded both sides of the civil war to lay down their weapons for two months, so their medical teams could treat those afflicted. The Carters and their team of experts then purified the water supplies (the disease was contracted through contaminated drinking water) and treated the sufferers. Thanks in part to the Carters' work, the Guinea worm disease was eradicated by 1996.

## CARTER WINS PRAISE—AND CRITICISM—FOR HIS WORK

For all of Carter's work for peace and humanitarianism, he has won the Gold Medal of the International Institute of Human Rights; the Martin Luther King Jr. Nonviolent Peace Prize; the Liberty Medal; the Presidential Medal of Freedom; and the Albert Schweitzer Prize for Humanitarianism. He has been nominated seven times for the Nobel Peace Prize (and many people believe that he should have won, particularly for his work on the Camp David Accord).

But Carter has also been criticized for some of his diplomacy. He is willing to discuss things with even the most hated and brutal leaders. In 1994 he negotiated with Radovan Karadzic and Ratko Mladic, Bosnian Serb leaders who were suspected war criminals. People were upset that he expressed sympathy for their cause. "The people who cause human rights abuses are the same ones who can stop them," Carter explained, "and if no one else will talk to them, I will. It's not only an opportunity, it's a responsibility." Rosalynn told *Time* that "Jimmy sees good in everybody, and sometimes he sees more than is there."

When Carter isn't building houses for Habitat for Humanity, or fighting diseases, or staving off wars, or writing, he might be found teaching his Sunday Bible school class at Maranatha Baptist Church, where he is also deacon.

Jimmy Carter's journey to communist Cuba in May of 2002 (see p. 14) was the first time a U.S. president, in *or* out of office, had set foot on the island since Fidel Castro's revolution in 1959. Representing the Carter Center, the former president saw in the historic visit an opportunity to share ideas on improving relations between that country and the United States. While there, Carter met with Castro himself and with many other Cubans from different walks of life. In a speech delivered at the University of Havana and televised throughout the island, Carter called for Cuba to "join the community of democracies"

President Bill Clinton awards the Presidential Medal of Freedom to Jimmy Carter in Atlanta in August of 1999. The Medal is the highest honor that the U.S. government can grant to a civilian.

and openly supported a petition, sponsored by Cuban dissidents, that demanded widespread government reforms. He criticized Castro's record on human rights but also spoke against the 40-year-old U.S. trade embargo against Cuba as a measure that most American did not support. While Carter conceded that his visit was unlikely to change Castro's policies, the former president's characteristic fair approach, openness, and direct style earned him praise from Cubans and Americans alike—even though some have claimed that he carries his diplomatic role as former president too far.

Many people wonder why Carter is so devoted to public service after leaving the Oval Office. Some critics think that he is trying to make up for his failings as a president, and they see his good works as a way to vindicate his presidency. But perhaps his reasoning is much simpler than that. His Christian faith has given him a strong sense of responsibility to others. "Since I was a young boy," he wrote, "the thrust of my prayers—at least when I was trying to make a good impression on God—has always been that I not fail to use fully and effectively the one life I have on earth."

And Carter continues to enjoy his work. He said of his life after the Oval Office: "I feel truer to myself. I'm more a missionary than a politician. I am really where I belong."

Jimmy Carter has single-handedly proven that there is life after the presidency. And still, he maintains, "I've not achieved all I set out to do; perhaps no one ever does."

| | |
|---|---|
| **1924** | James Earl Carter Jr. is born in Plains, Georgia, on October 1. |
| **1941–42** | Attends Georgia Southwestern College. |
| **1942–43** | Attends Georgia Institute of Technology. |
| **1943–46** | Attends United States Naval Academy and graduates 59th in a class of 820. |
| **1946** | Marries Rosalynn Smith on July 7. |
| **1946–53** | Serves in the United States Navy. |
| **1947** | Son John William (Jack) is born. |
| **1950** | Son James Earl III (Chip) is born. |
| **1952** | Son Donnel Jeffrey (Jeff) is born. |
| **1953–77** | Owns and operates peanut farm and warehouse in Plains, Georgia. |
| **1962** | Elected state senator. |
| **1967** | Daughter Amy Lynn is born. |
| **1970** | Elected governor of Georgia. |
| **1976** | Defeats Gerald Ford in presidential election on November 2. |
| **1977** | Sworn in as 39th president of the United States on January 20; pardons most evaders of the Vietnam draft the next day. |
| **1977** | On February 24, announces that United States will reduce foreign aid to three nations because of their violations of human rights. |
| **1978** | Congress ratifies two Panama Canal treaties on April 18. |
| **1978** | Between September 5 and September 17, conducts talks at Camp David with Israeli Prime Minister Menachem Begin and Egyptian President Anwar Sadat. |
| **1979** | United States normalizes diplomatic relations with the People's Republic of China on January 1. |
| **1979** | On March 26, Menachem Begin and Anwar Sadat sign the Camp David Accord. |
| **1979** | President Carter and Premier Leonid Brezhnev sign SALT II on June 18. |
| **1979** | Iranian students storm the U.S. embassy in Tehran on November 4 and take 52 Americans hostage. |
| **1980** | Authorizes mission to rescue hostages on April 24; mission is aborted, and eight serviceman die in crash. |

**1980**  Ronald Reagan defeats Jimmy Carter in landslide victory on November 4.

**1980**  Congress ratifies the Alaska Lands Bill on December 2.

**1981**  As Ronald Reagan is sworn in as the 40th president of the United States—January 20—Iran releases the American hostages.

**1982**  Founds the Carter Center of Emory University.

**1991**  Launches the Atlanta Project.

**1994**  Acting as an unofficial diplomat, Carter meets with North Korean President Kim Il Sung in June and convinces him to end their nuclear weapons program.

**1994**  Negotiates with Haitian leaders in September, helping to prevent U.S. military intervention.

# FURTHER READING

Abernathy, M. Glenn. *The Carter Years: The President and Policy Making.* New York: St. Martin's Press, 1984.

Carter, Jimmy. *Always a Reckoning.* New York: Times Books, 1995

Carter, Jimmy. *An Hour Before Daylight.* New York: Simon & Schuster, 2001.

Carter, Jimmy. *Living Faith.* New York: Times Books, 1996.

Carter, Jimmy. *Talking Peace.* New York: Dutton, 1993.

Carter, Jimmy. *Turning Point: A Candidate, a State, and a Nation Coming of Age.* New York: Times Books, 1992.

Carter, Jimmy. *Why Not the Best?* Nashville, Tennessee: Broadman Press, 1975.

Carter, Jimmy, and Rosalynn Carter. *Everything to Gain.* New York: Random House, 1987.

Carter, Jimmy. "The Best Years of Our Lives." *Business Week,* July 20, 1998, p.112.

Carter, Jimmy. "President Jimmy Carter Takes Issue with an Editorial." *U.S. News & World Report,* October 31, 1994, Volume 117, issue 17, p.10.

Chambers, John Whiteclay. "Jimmy Carter's Public Policy Ex-Presidency." *Political Science Quarterly,* Fall 1998.

"Give Her Shelter." *People,* December 19, 1994, Volume 42, issue 25, p.76.

Kiefer, Francine. "A Meeting of America's Most Exclusive Trade Union." *Christian Science Monitor,* May 11, 2000, p. 4.

McPherson, James M, general editor. *"To The Best of My Ability": The American Presidents.* New York: Dorling Kindersley Publishing, 2000.


The Carter Center
*www.cartercenter.org*

Brinkley, Douglas. *The Unfinished Presidency: Jimmy Carter's Journey Beyond the White House.* New York: Viking, 1998.

Carter, Jimmy. *Keeping Faith: Memoirs of a President.* New York: Bantam Books, 1982.

Church, George J. "One Very Busy Ex-Prez." *Time,* October 3, 1994, Volume 144, issue 14, p. 36.

Kramer, Jerome. "Jimmy Carter: Man of his Words." *Book,* November/December 2001, pp. 31–37.

Lazo, Caroline. *Jimmy Carter: On the Road to Peace.* Parsippany, New Jersey: Dillon Press, 1996.

Olson, Tod. "America Held Hostage." *Scholastic Update,* May 11, 1998, Volume 130, issue 14, p. 20.

Schleier, Curt. "Jimmy Carter, Former President of the United States." *Biography,* July 1997, Volume 1, issue 7, p.76.

Smith, Gary, and Harry Benson. "What Makes Jimmy Run?" *Life,* November 1995, Volume 18, issue 13, p.100.

page:

| | | | |
|---|---|---|---|
| 2: | AP/Wide World Photos | 60: | AP/Wide World Photos |
| 11: | 21st Century Publishing | 62: | AP/Wide World Photos |
| 12: | AP/Wide World Photos | 65: | AP/Wide World Photos |
| 14: | AP/Wide World Photos | 69: | AP/Wide World Photos |
| 16: | AP/Wide World Photos | 72: | Bettmann/Corbis |
| 19: | AP/Wide World Photos | 74: | Corbis |
| 22: | Corbis | 79: | AP/Wide World Photos |
| 26: | Corbis | 82: | Corbis |
| 28: | Lowell Georgia/Corbis | 84: | Bettmann/Corbis |
| 32: | AP/Wide World Photos | 87: | 21st Century Publishing |
| 35 | AP/Wide World Photos | 90: | David Rubinger/Corbis |
| 38: | Corbis | 92: | AP/Wide World Photos |
| 42: | AP/Wide World Photos | 97: | Corbis |
| 45: | BettmannCorbis | 101: | Bettmann/Corbis |
| 47: | AP/Wide World Photos | 102: | AP/Wide World Photos |
| 50: | AP/Wide World Photos | 104: | AP/Wide World Photos |
| 53: | AP/Wide World Photos | 109: | AP/Wide World Photos |
| 59: | AP/Wide World Photos | 114: | AP/Wide World Photos |

Cover: © Bettmann/Corbis

**KERRY ACKER** is a freelance writer and editor based in Brooklyn, New York. Some of her other books include *The Kids Fun-Filled Encyclopedia* and *Backyard Animals* (both published by Kidsbooks), *Everything You Need to Know about the Goth Scene* (Rosen Publishing), and *The Millennium Journal* (Andrews McMeel). She holds a bachelor's degree in English literature and Spanish from the College of the Holy Cross in Worcester, Massachusetts.

**ARTHUR M. SCHLESINGER, JR.** is the leading American historian of our time. He won the Pulitzer Prize for his book *The Age of Jackson* (1945) and again for a chronicle of the Kennedy Administration, *A Thousand Days* (1965), which also won the National Book Award. Professor Schlesinger is the Albert Schweitzer Professor of the Humanities at the City University of New York and has been involved in several other Chelsea House projects, including the series REVOLUTIONARY WAR LEADERS, COLONIAL LEADERS, and YOUR GOVERNMENT.